GOD'S BELOVED

GOD'S BELOVED

*A Spiritual Biography
of Henri Nouwen*

MICHAEL O'LAUGHLIN

ORBIS BOOKS

Maryknoll, New York 10545

Founded in 1970, Orbis Books endeavors to publish works that enlighten the mind, nourish the spirit, and challenge the conscience. The publishing arm of the Maryknoll Fathers and Brothers, Orbis seeks to explore the global dimensions of the Christian faith and mission, to invite dialogue with diverse cultures and religious traditions, and to serve the cause of reconciliation and peace. The books published reflect the views of their authors and do not represent the official position of the Maryknoll Society. To learn more about Maryknoll and Orbis Books, please visit our website at www.maryknoll.org.

Library of Congress Cataloging-in-Publication Data

O'Laughlin, Michael.
  God's beloved : a spiritual biography of Henri Nouwen / Michael O'Laughlin.
    p. cm.
  Includes bibliographical references (p.   ).
  ISBN 1-57075-561-2 (pbk.)
  1. Nouwen, Henri J. M. I. Title.
  BX4705.N87O43 2004
  282'.092—dc22
                    2004006509

For Robert A. Jonas and Peter Weiskel

I would like to remember more, so that my own little history could be a book to reflect on and learn from. I don't believe that my life is a long row of randomly chained incidents and accidents of which I am not much more than a passive victim. No, I think that nothing is accidental but that God molded me through the events of my life and that I am called to recognize his molding hand and praise him in gratitude for the great things he has done to me.

Henri Nouwen
The Genesee Diary

CONTENTS

ACKNOWLEDGMENTS

This book is the fruit of many conversations with many people and my reading of the books and memorials written about Henri Nouwen since his death. Although I have learned something from every book and every person I have talked with, I want to dedicate this book to Robert A. Jonas and Peter Weiskel, because I have learned more about Henri Nouwen talking to these two friends of mine, and of his, than I have from any other source. In many ways, I see this book as another installment in a continuing conversation with Robert and with Peter, and with the many other people who have tried to understand Henri Nouwen better and absorb his special teaching.

Henri was a very lovable guy, and I suppose that is one reason why we are all still so caught up with him and his message. I do know that there are many people who will read this book because of their sincere love for Henri, and I want to acknowledge how much solidarity I feel with them. Folks, we have a Nouwen Centre, and a Nouwen Society, but perhaps what we really need is an "I Love Henri" Club to complete the picture! I send you my warmest greetings.

I also want to acknowledge the special help I have received. I was the recipient of writing grants from both the Nouwen Centre and the U.S. Nouwen Society that helped free me up at a crucial stage in writing this book. I also want to thank my mother, Alice O'Laughlin, and Robert Cox for loaning me books and for help with some of the psychological components of the book. Laurent Nouwen gave me valuable information regarding his family and Louis ter Steeg made some helpful comments regarding Henri's life in Holland, for which I am very grateful. Fr. John Cockayne volunteered to be the book's first reader. Finally, I want to say thanks to Robert Ellsberg and all the staff at Orbis Books who have done so much to make books of this kind available to all of us.

INTRODUCTION

The Nouwen Phenomenon

Henri Nouwen, the Dutch priest and spiritual writer, died in 1996. Although his name never became a household word, at the time of his death he could be counted as one of the most popular Catholic writers anywhere. Indeed, he was read not only by Catholics, or only by speakers of English, but by every sort of Christian in communities all around the globe. He achieved remarkable recognition for an author of religious books. For instance, when then first-lady Hillary Clinton was asked by Oprah Winfrey to recommend a *single* book to her "O" magazine readers, she chose a Nouwen title that she said had helped her through her darkest hours in the White House.[1]

Nouwen's books addressed spiritual issues, such as prayer and ministry, as well as problems that were more existential, such as solitude and the divide between rich and poor. He was also perpetually writing his own life story, through either published journals or by recounting his spiritual experiences. Even in his books on broader spiritual issues, most of the examples he used came from his own life. By choosing this style of writing, he left nothing in the abstract. Everything he said was brought down to earth and made personal. As Nouwen wrote more and more about his experiences, his choices and his concerns, his own life became a big part of his message. Henri Nouwen's books and his life constantly overlapped and intertwined. In the end, his life of writing spiritual books became its own book, one that we can "read" and from which we can learn a great deal.

The contours of Nouwen's life were indeed interesting. Although he became a well-known spiritual writer, Nouwen did not embrace the lifestyle of a media-savvy author or pundit. In fact, he declined most of the many speaking invitations he received, and he abandoned his academic appointments, first at Yale, then at Harvard, in order to seek a more clearly spiritual way of life. His first radical step in this direction was to immerse himself in the meditative silence of a Cistercian monastery. Later, he went to the Third World to live as a missionary and worked in a shantytown near Lima, Peru.

While both of these experiences broadened his outlook and added new dimensions to his writing and teaching, Henri Nouwen did not find what he was seeking in either of these settings. He longed for some more satisfying form of life and ministry that would ground him spiritually and give him the feeling of having "arrived home." Nouwen was searching for some place or situation that might offer him intimacy, continuity, and acceptance.

It might seem odd that a famous priest and author could seek a place where he would feel accepted. However, Henri Nouwen was dogged by an undercurrent of emotional uncertainty that none of his very real achievements could completely relieve or erase. Henri Nouwen searched openly for something that perhaps many long for secretly—friendship and real intimacy with other people and with God.

Most of those who knew Nouwen in the period of his most intense searching, as I did, regarded his restless spiritual pilgrimage as one more dimension of his unique personality. However, a deeper analysis would perhaps have revealed something more: Henri Nouwen was waiting for a call, which is always a trying and difficult experience. All the signs were there: Nouwen would move off in some new and promising direction, only to return intrigued and better informed, but disappointed. He sometimes wondered if he would have to create from the ground up the community he was seeking. As his frustration grew, so too did the honing of his objective. Nouwen, through trial and error, was actually coming to a better understanding of his own needs and of God's will for his life. In fact, the options he had already tried—being a university professor, or becoming a monk or a missionary—cannot be considered particularly inspired choices. They were all standard paths often taken by people in the Church. The monastery and the missions were options that had satisfied the cravings of many spiritually unsatisfied people in the past. These options came highly recommended, but they did not work for Henri Nouwen. He was unique, and standard solutions did not fit his case.

The solution, when it came, was a complete surprise, as is often the case when God intervenes in someone's life. Nouwen's desire was primarily for a spiritual home. This desire was fulfilled in 1985, as he was growing more uncomfortable with his position at Harvard University. After some preliminary contacts, he was invited to become the chaplain to Daybreak, a community near Toronto. Daybreak is part of l'Arche, an international ecumenical community centered on persons with mental and physical disabilities, who are known as "core members." This was a community that was living, as Nouwen wrote after meeting them, "in the spirit of the Beatitudes." He was intrigued by l'Arche, but he didn't immediately realize that l'Arche was the answer to his prayers. Even though Nouwen had a niece who was handicapped, he had never considered the possibility that he might one day find himself in ministry with handicapped people.

However, Daybreak is a very special place. The sight of college students who had volunteered to spend a year of their lives living with people who were mentally and physically disabled

seemed like an embodiment of Nouwen's own teaching on embracing a life of less "success" and more meaning. Likewise, he
was disarmed by the open affection and vulnerability of the core
members. It was clear that they were responsible for l'Arche's
special atmosphere of compassion and intimacy. He realized
that these wounded people had their own essential ministry. He
would often claim that they were able to create community
wherever they went!

He was also at first secretly, and then openly, pleased and
surprised by the community's acceptance of him as a person.
There was no need in l'Arche for him to live up to people's expectations of him as a famous teacher or guru, because in
l'Arche no one thought in those terms. Again, the core members, who could not have read any of Nouwen's books even if
they had wanted to, created an atmosphere that was markedly
more Christian than that usually found in the outside world.

When Henri Nouwen was invited to serve as chaplain at
Daybreak, he interpreted the invitation as a spiritual call. He
accepted that call and moved from Boston to Toronto. The
first period he spent there was devoted to adjustment and
learning. Nouwen was asked to live in a community house and
perform all of the routine chores and daily tasks that living
with the handicapped entails. He took care of the most handicapped of Daybreak's members—a "hands-on" experience if
ever there was one.

It was a very absorbing and purifying experience. There
were many difficulties and he realized he was very, very far from
his former life in academia. Nouwen, a man of words, was confronted with persons who could not understand words. A man
of action, he was confronted by persons who could barely move
their arms and legs. He became more centered. Living within
l'Arche, Nouwen was able to more successfully resist both the
pull of invitations to speak to large groups of people and the su-

perficial and supposedly glamorous life that even small-time celebrity usually entails. Instead of pursuing wider popularity, he devoted himself to the community and to friendship and to ministry to individuals, both within l'Arche and elsewhere.

A Man with Many Friends

A peculiar ability to befriend others was one of most remarkable and appealing traits of Henri Nouwen. He was able to connect on a personal level to literally hundreds, and even thousands of people. Focused, animated, sincere and generous, he made himself very available to others. He habitually went out of his way to make individual people feel special and appreciated. He seemed able to draw on some deep inner wellspring of energy as he cared for them. Through visits, letters, phone calls, and packages, Nouwen became a dear friend and trusted advisor to more people than can be counted. Wherever he happened to be living, the local florist experienced a sudden and dramatic increase in business as that shop became an extension of Nouwen's one-man goodwill ministry.

It was almost as if Henri Nouwen was living two remarkable lives at the same time. Perhaps it was even or three or four. Insightful and prolific as a writer, he was also one of the great preachers and teachers of his generation. In addition, remarkable things often seemed to happen in his encounters with other people. The one-on-one meetings he had and the relationships he developed became illuminating and liberating experiences for Nouwen's friends and followers, as was shown by the flood of tributes that have been shared and published since his death.[2]

One of the best-documented examples of the unusual relationships Henri Nouwen had is this one: In 1980, when he was a professor at Yale University, Nouwen was interviewed by a young reporter sent to write a brief story about him for a magazine. Before the interview had proceeded very far, Nouwen reversed the normal question/answer protocol and began questioning and giving pastoral advice to the reporter, who happened to be a very cynical and secular Jewish New Yorker.

Learning how discouraged and frustrated the young writer was, Nouwen challenged him to give up his job doing little interviews and devote himself to writing the novel he longed to write. When the young man explained the practical impossibility of doing this, Nouwen proposed a dramatic solution—he invited him to move to Yale. Nouwen said he would find the money so that this young writer, whose name was Fred Bratman, could give his novel a try.

Thus began a special friendship between two men who had very little in common. Initially, it was very difficult for Bratman to accept Nouwen's enormous generosity to him, a stranger, and he questioned Nouwen's motives. In the end, Bratman could only conclude that Henri Nouwen treated people in a way that was different from what normally might be expected.[3] The two carried on an interesting exchange. Despite the differences in their perspectives, Bratman and Nouwen continued to meet and enjoy each other's company after Bratman returned to New York and Nouwen moved on as well. Nouwen wrote one of his seminal books, *Life of the Beloved*, for Fred Bratman.

Although he was raised and trained within the narrow confines of Dutch Catholicism, Nouwen's experience of Vatican II and his employment in Protestant divinity schools stretched his boundaries substantially. His relationships with people like Fred Bratman extended his perspective even further. He was coming slowly to see that not only God but even Christ himself was greater than Christianity, and that through Christ all people are graced with God's favor. *Life of the Beloved* was a bold attempt to express these new insights.

The relationship he fostered with Fred Bratman was not unique or unusual for Henri Nouwen. He was constantly reaching out in new directions and readjusting his theology as he did so. One of his most popular books was entitled *Reaching Out*,[4] and these words sum up a basic hallmark of his spirituality. While part of his outgoing ministry to others simply sprang from his own personality, there was also an unmistakable Christian or Christ-like character to his energetic encounter with people everywhere.

I believe this was an important part of his great giftedness and his ministry. As he moved out beyond the boundaries of his training and experience, Nouwen never divested himself of his decidedly Christian outlook and identity. In fact, Henri Nouwen related to others on a level that drove his readers and those around him to think about the attitudes and stories at the heart of the Christian gospel. Although Henri Nouwen was not the sort of Christian who is constantly quoting from the Bible, in whatever he was doing—whether preaching or eating or driving a car—the gospel was never far away. He seemed to be living it. To many of the people who met him, he appeared to be a veritable beacon of light. Indeed, he embodied the Catholic theory of priesthood expressed in the words *alter Christus*. He was like another Christ.

A Man Acquainted with Sorrow

Yet if Nouwen was "another Christ," he was also a man of sorrows walking his own personal *via dolorosa*. The gifts that God gave him helped others, but apparently did not afford him any great solace. Even after he became part of l'Arche, he was still restless, uncertain, and, occasionally, even unable to cope. Capable of greatness as a speaker, a writer and a counselor, he remained oddly incapable of performing simple tasks that normal people do every day (such as making a sandwich!). Like a number of celebrities and other very talented people, Nouwen was uniquely gifted but also uniquely needy.

Other persons with similar combinations of talents and limitations simply hire enough staff to keep their practical incompetence or emotional shortcomings from becoming public knowledge. Henri Nouwen certainly had a lot of helpers who kept his operation going, but he did not hire people in order to camouflage his impractical or insecure side. Instead, he chose to live in a labor-intensive, hands-on environment alongside handicapped persons, in a community where no one was exempt from doing the chores. In l'Arche he was forced to face his incompetence and learn to cope with it. It was a measure of his remarkable humility that he would take on a lifestyle filled with menial tasks at a time in life when he could have avoided them. Through the trials of life in community he was also able to arrive at a deeper level of emotional stability.

Growing Recognition

This was the Henri Nouwen who was known, loved, and widely appreciated at the time of his death: a writer, a priest, and a spiritual friend and guide to hundreds and thousands. Since then, however, another phenomenon has occurred. Henri Nouwen has not merely been missed, as all people are after they die. Instead, those who knew him have had a growing sense that Nouwen was a very special person, not merely a great writer and loving friend, but someone sent to the Christian community by God. A small flood of books, either about Henri Nouwen or based on his writings, have appeared. In addition, there have been articles, films, seminars, retreats, and an international teleconference, all on Henri Nouwen. There are now Henri Nouwen societies in the United States, Canada, the Netherlands, and even Chile. There is a Nouwen archive at the University of Toronto and a Henri Nouwen Literary Centre. Something important seems to be happening. At the very least, there is now a whole new chapter to be written on Nouwen's legacy.

This book is very much about living in that "Nouwen legacy." Like others perhaps, I want to learn all I can from the one person I have known who seemed sent into this world with a special grace and message from God. However, I have found that not every aspect of following in Nouwen's footsteps has been easy or completely straightforward. Henri Nouwen was unique enough as a person that his way of living might be admired, but it can hardly be embraced by anyone other than another Henri Nouwen. One then turns to his teachings to find something about prayer, about community, and about living—a message relevant for our lives.

Understanding Henri

Frankly, I keep coming back to Henri himself. I have very much needed to understand him better. He was clearly a special sort of person, at once wonderful and perplexing. Indeed, one of the most important yet problematic tasks of the Nouwen legacy has been the creation of an accurate portrait of the man. The difficulty of creating this portrait is due in part to the complexity of his personality and to the subtle yet powerful working of God's hand in Henri Nouwen's most remarkable life and ministry. It is not easy to sort out and separate those aspects of his story that are part of Nouwen's personal psychology from others that spring from the fundamentals of Christian ministry and spirituality.

Several highly qualified writers have already attempted this task, which is made more difficult by the fact that anyone who writes about Henri Nouwen must have a good background in theology, psychology, and spirituality, and must be able to keep these different perspectives in balance. The first written attempt to understand Henri Nouwen's life and message was made by a Protestant pastor in Holland. Jurjen Beumer's *Henri Nouwen: A Restless Seeking for God*[5] comments on Nouwen's life and background and maps out the many areas in which he contributed to an understanding of spirituality. When this book first appeared in Dutch, I remember Henri telling me happily that not only was he writing books, but books were now being written about him! He felt very flattered, of course.

After Henri Nouwen died, the need for a book that grappled with who he was was felt immediately. The most notable of those that appeared was written by the British theology student and journalist Michael Ford. His book, *Wounded Prophet: A Portrait of Henri J. M. Nouwen*,[6] is the most penetrating treatment of Nouwen to emerge thus far. Almost an exposé, *Wounded Prophet* caused something of a sensation when it first appeared, for it revealed Nouwen's homosexual orientation, a personal secret shared with only a few sympathetic friends while Nouwen was alive. *Wounded Prophet* was based on interviews with family and close friends of Nouwen in the year after his death. Because of the sources employed and the period when these people were consulted, the book also reflects the feelings of loss and confusion felt by a community struggling to understand the flaws and limitations of one of the most wonderful but sometimes maddening persons they had ever known.

Wounded Prophet makes a sustained attempt to get beyond the warm appreciation that most of Nouwen's friends felt for him to focus on the shortcomings and the psychology of Henri Nouwen. Michael Ford is honest and penetrating in his evaluation of Nouwen, but nevertheless *Wounded Prophet* has not been universally accepted as a faithful portrait of "Henri." The book is not an entirely accurate portrayal of Nouwen, mostly because of its negative assessment of Nouwen's psychological health. The Nouwen of *Wounded Healer* is calculating and manipulative, more crippled than wounded. In my estimation and that of a number of others, this is not what Nouwen was really like.[7] However, no other book has provided as much information and dealt with the difficult issues of Henri Nouwen's life as directly as has *Wounded Prophet*.

A briefer but more trustworthy portrait of Nouwen was created shortly after his death by his friend and confidante, Robert Jonas. Jonas was working as a psychotherapist at the time he knew Nouwen, and he continues to counsel people today as a spiritual director. Due to issues relating to confidentiality, Jonas was unwilling to detail any of the more sensitive aspects of Nouwen's story and personality, but he does sketch out an overall picture of Henri Nouwen, including some treatment of his more problematic personal traits. The Henri Nouwen he presents is a gifted minister, and the importance of Jesus in Henri's life is given appropriate space and prominence. His book, part of the "Modern Spiritual Masters Series" from Orbis Books, is simply called *Henri Nouwen*.[8]

Deirdre LaNoue, from Dallas Baptist University, wrote her doctoral thesis on Henri Nouwen, and that thesis appeared in book form in 2000. Because her book was originally produced for academic review, it provides some of the most complete factual information and the most extensive bibliography of any book written about Henri Nouwen. She sums up his thinking and gives some suggestions on where we might go in developing his spirituality. Her book is called *The Spiritual Legacy of Henri Nouwen*.[9]

My own book has taken shape in part as a reaction to reading Michael Ford's *Wounded Prophet*. I feel indebted to Ford for having clearly sensed and articulated both the promise and the problems of a Nouwen spirituality, and I think his book is the starting point for any serious consideration of Henri Nouwen at this time. However, Ford did not know Henri well, and his portrait of him, particularly of his psychology, invites further inquiry and development. Nouwen certainly had psychological problems that fed into, as well as limited, his genius. However, knowing that he had psychological problems is not the key to understanding Henri Nouwen.

I believe there was some greater factor at play. The strange but undeniable truth regarding Henri Nouwen is that simply by being himself, he changed the way Christianity is practiced in the Western world. This may seem an impossibly large claim to make, putting Nouwen in the same category with persons such as C. S. Lewis in Britain, Billy Graham or Thomas Merton in the United States, or Romano Guardini in continental Europe. Yet it is true: as modern Christians loosened up and became more personal, more humble, and more ecumenical, as Vatican II thinking took hold among Catholics, as we all refocused on Jesus and scripture, Henri Nouwen came to symbolize the important ways in which things were changing and where things were going.

Remarkably, he did this simply by holding fast to the heart of Christian experience, and by speaking frankly about his own doubts and limitations. He did not create an up-to-date, intellectually respectable theology to be disseminated and discussed in university classrooms and among churchy intellectuals. Rather, he wrote books that purposely set aside intellectual issues. He wrote plainly and he spoke to the heart. What he created was an inspired vision of active and inquisitive faith, fashioned within his own brokenness and openness to God. Ronald Rolheiser, who dedicated his book, *Holy Longing*, to Nouwen, put it this way:

[He was] our generation's Kierkegaard. By sharing his own struggles, he mentored us all, helping us to pray while not knowing how to pray, to rest while feeling restless, to be at peace while tempted, to feel safe while still anxious, to be surrounded by a cloud of light while still in darkness, and to love while still in doubt.[10]

As Rolheiser notes, Nouwen's faith, his message, was one adapted to a world where certainties had failed. He lived and worked in an era when established authorities of all kinds were under clouds of suspicion or doubt. As the modern, more disconnected lifestyle, the increase in secular thinking, and wave after wave of scientific discoveries beat upon and eroded the once rock-like certainties and religious practices of earlier generations, many Christians were driven to doubt and distrust. Large numbers left their fellowships, their convents, the priesthood, and even their churches.

Those believers who remained found a way forward that was based not on certainty or on any previous confessional insularity. Neither was it based on the myth of science or on the popular convictions of secular humanism. The Christianity that emerged from the cultural shifts of the latter half of the twentieth century was based on a new level of informed involvement, of honesty and of openness, even openness to doubt. The ages during which Christian faith was often based on conformity, memorized beliefs, ignorance, or even fearful superstition were past. In this difficult time of transition, as the Christianity of the Western world burned to the ground and rose from its own ashes, Nouwen provided a model for many. He opened up a narrow pathway in the darkness, showing how one could live in a way faithful to the Christian gospel when much of society, the world, and the Church had changed completely.

Charism

I believe there was some kind of charism at work in Nouwen's life and ministry. It was not that Henri Nouwen was in tune with his times. Rather, it was that a lot of people during those times were in tune with Henri Nouwen. What I mean is that the way in which Christianity is practiced evolved to a new form due partly to the intensity, the freedom, the love, and the authenticity that Henri Nouwen brought to his ministry of writing and witness. He was not a saintly figure, like a Mother Teresa or a Dalai Lama. Instead, Nouwen was one of us, more a layman than a priest in his outlook, another imperfect, questioning believer in Jesus. Nouwen once suggested that his middle initials, "J. M.," stood for "just me,"[11] and this sums up his sense of self precisely. He lived his life as an Everyman. He tried to speak to each person he met on his or her level, as a friend, and thus he reached out and touched people from every station of life, one by one.

I recently met a man named Michael Flood, a retired Irish janitor, who believes that Henri Nouwen's ministry and prayers cured him of cancer. The story Michael Flood told me was like many others I have heard. In typical Nouwen fashion, when Henri learned that Flood, someone he had never met, was going through a life-threatening crisis and had expressed a desire to learn more about Christianity, he didn't simply write him a short pastoral note. He reached out and befriended him. The two men corresponded at length and spent time together. When one of Flood's friends asked him why "a great man like Henri Nouwen would want to spend time with a shit-kicking janitor like *you*," Flood had the perfect answer ready for him, and delivered it with an Irish lilt: "If you can ask that question, it just shows how little you know about Henri Nouwen!" Nouwen promised Flood he would offer a special prayer for

Flood as he held up the chalice during the Eucharist, a prayer for his healing. Indeed, Michael Flood did experience a remission of his cancer that may have been miraculous, and he believes that his healing was granted because of Nouwen's prayer.

This relationship with Michael Flood was one of hundreds of relationships that Nouwen entered into and that sometimes led to profound experiences of growth and healing for those he met and befriended. It was as if some special grace or luminosity emanated from him when he was with people. He was really a "man of God." This was what the prophets were called in ancient Israel. Henri was like them. He had the gift.

As I write now, almost eight years after his death, Henri Nouwen is still a mystery and a source of inspiration to me. I still have a need, which I think is shared by many others, to know and understand what was special about Henri Nouwen. What does his life mean in spiritual terms? What should I or anyone else do to continue Henri Nouwen's spiritual legacy?

Nouwen was indeed a bearer of the Word who continues to be heard by Christians in many parts of the world. But, as the Epistle of James reminds us,[12] to merely hear the Word without attempting to *do* anything in response, without attempting to live within that Word, is to become a spiritual failure. It is to die, in some small measure, rather than to grow and live. So the Nouwen legacy, if it is to be a living tradition, must go beyond merely reading books by Henri Nouwen. Certainly we would like to understand him better, but ultimately we must find ways to show others, as Henri Nouwen showed us, that there is something here that reveals the ways of God. The message must be absorbed and lived.

Of course, one may still ask if it is really profitable for anyone to spend time thinking about Nouwen, or about any other person from the past, no matter how great or influential. Is not Christianity, especially as Henri Nouwen expressed it, all about being present to God in any given moment? How can we be authentic or even fully "present" if we are thinking about somebody else?

It is true that we must learn how to enter the realm of the heart where we are alone with God, and not thinking about other people. However, as soon as we try to teach ourselves to do this, or try to achieve any real spiritual insight, we fall in line behind those who have gone before us and become heirs to a tradition. We discover for ourselves the truth that the Christian faith is not something we invent or that we are the first to discover. Rather, it is passed down from one person to another and shared. As faith is communicated, it expands, grows, and is changed. This is one thing that can surely be said about Henri Nouwen—he made important expansions and adjustments to the faith he received. Henri Nouwen took further what he learned from others, and we must do the same with what he has given us.

This Book's Purpose

This book is a spiritual biography. Now what exactly does that mean? In the present case I have not tried to write a birth-to-death chronological narrative, although I do include some reflection on the shape and meaning of Henri's life. I have tried to see Henri's life and his teachings in spiritual terms, and to explore those areas that I feel are most important. More than anything else, I want to search out some of the less explored aspects of Nouwen's life, the ones that are most pertinent to a better assessment of him.

I begin with his formative years, including where he came from, because I think this is essential to seeing how much of Nouwen's special brilliance and special concerns were due to his origins and early environment. Then I turn to the psychology of Henri Nouwen. Many people have referred to Nouwen as a complex figure. I think it is time to delve a little deeper, and see what particular psychological issues were most problematic for Nouwen. Indeed, I believe there were specific issues at the heart of Nouwen's famous unease, and even his personality, and these also must be considered before we can take proper stock of this man. I believe, in fact, that not only was Nouwen troubled by identifiable psychological issues, he did a good deal to address these and work through them, which is all the more reason to consider his life as a model for others.

The next issue is related. Henri Nouwen's approach to spirituality was certainly unique and personal, yet perhaps it can be better appreciated if its form and style are better understood. Nouwen's way of speaking and writing grew out of an awareness that I feel is more typically artistic than theological. What place did art play in Nouwen's life? Several writers and visual artists had an enormous influence on Henri, and perhaps the artist's way of seeing and creating became Nouwen's way of doing spirituality.

In the last three chapters of the book, I explore a few themes that are central to Nouwen and his legacy. Some of these themes he purposely developed. Others are apparent when we take a longer view of his interests and his development. While there are over a dozen topics on which Nouwen wrote a book or a series of articles, in which he took an interest or helped us to see things more clearly, we should not allow his many interests to obscure the fact that he made a lasting contribution to Christian thinking and practice regarding a few central issues: these are the Eucharist, Jesus, and the spiritual life. I devote a chapter to each of these subjects.

There are, then, six main chapters to this book. The first half of the book concerns three important aspects of Henri Nouwen's life, aspects that I believe help us the most to understand him better. The second half of the book focuses on three topics on which he made a great contribution to our thinking and living as a community of faith. While this book is certainly about Henri Nouwen, I hope that the question of how we might learn from his life and teachings will never be far from us.

I honestly believe that we have now reached an important stage as readers, or listeners, or admirers, or friends of Nouwen. We no longer are in need of commemorations or memoirs, especially since there have been some beautiful ones created by many of his friends. Now I think the time has come to revisit some of the exciting—and some of the perplexing—aspects of his life and personality and try to assess him more carefully. Then let us go on to ask ourselves what we have learned from him, or what we still need to learn from this man who was certainly unique, and whom many have come to regard as a prophet.

In this book I want to do more than simply present information about Henri Nouwen. My hope is to begin a process in which we place ourselves in the unfinished story of God's Spirit. There may be lessons that Henri Nouwen has yet to teach us, and these lessons will be more about how we live *our* lives than about how he lived his.

1
ORIGINS AND EARLY INFLUENCES

A Dutchman

Henri Nouwen was born in the Netherlands in 1932. Holland is a special country, especially with regard to matters of religion. The Dutch spirit is determined in part by its size and position in Europe, especially its latitude and its openness to the sea. The Dutch are an enterprising, commercial people. They have been mariners and traders for centuries. They left their mark on the world, but in a way different way from that of the great imperial powers such as France, England, Spain, or Portugal. The Dutch sailed the world in search of trade, and most of their far-flung colonies were originally either islands or ports. Through commercial ventures such as the Dutch East India Company, Holland established lucrative colonies and trading posts that grew into important cities. Both Cape Town and New York were originally Dutch trading settlements.

At home, the coastal merchant mentality of the Dutch led to the formation of a more tolerant society than elsewhere in Europe. The Dutch shores became a refuge for religious dissidents, especially non-conformist Protestants and Jews. The dissidents and exiles who came to Holland from other parts of Europe often brought with them strongly held religious beliefs. Holland became a center for Anabaptists, for Puritans, for Jews, and especially for Calvinists. These groups formed self-sufficient enclaves in the Netherlands, and contact between different groups was primarily commercial. The character of these communities could be quite conservative, as well as religious. However, the different groups did live together in peace, which is more than can be said for such groups in other parts of Europe.

Tales of religious tension and violence in Holland's history can usually be traced to outside imperialist powers, such as the Hapsburgs or the Spanish, both of whom held Holland for long periods. The Dutch population itself seems, in historical perspective, to have been less bellicose. There is an additional reason why this might have been the case, namely, that the more uncompromising or fanatical Dutch religious groups and individuals abandoned Holland for America, Africa, or elsewhere. The best example of religious extremists who left Holland and settled elsewhere is the Boer population in South Africa.

The defining image of Holland is then of a commercial people. In fact, they have sometimes been called a "nation of shopkeepers." They were certainly intent on business expansion around the world in the colonial period, and Rotterdam is still the busiest port in Europe. Those who settled in Holland kept to their own communities and all prospered. Prosperity came naturally, for the Dutch people are hard working, inquisitive, and educated. Thus, the nation of Holland has long exhibited two characteristics later to be shared with much of modern culture—it has the bourgeois self-assuredness and business acumen derived from financial skill and resources, and it has a liberality derived from life in a pluralistic country of enlightenment, travel, and education.

If we look at Dutch history from a spiritual perspective, we see a nation preserving a careful balance. The dynamism of commerce, trade, and travel promoted personal and spiritual independence. Holland became an officially Protestant country very early on, and Protestantism became an important part of its ethos. On the other hand, the intellectual acumen of the Dutch and their conservatism held the spirit of dynamism and independence in check. This careful balance is well illustrated by a sixteenth-century figure, the Dutch scholar Erasmus, who had such a dramatic impact on Europe with his biblical scholarship that some people have said that Erasmus laid the egg that Luther hatched. However, Erasmus never broke with the Catholic Church. His Dutch character kept him in balance, even as the foundations of religious life in Europe shook with the aftershocks of a revolution he himself helped to start.

Over time, the compartmentalization of Holland into separate religious communities became an increasingly distinctive characteristic of Dutch life. Although there was no open hostility between them, different religious groups lived under a self-imposed "confessional apartheid."[1] As a consequence, instead of gravitating toward an open public social sphere, people's lives in Holland revolved around their family and its extended circle, called a *kring*. By the time Henri Nouwen was born, there were separate banks, clubs, businesses, schools, political parties, newspapers, and, of course, churches for each of the different *zuilen*, the "columns," or communities, of Dutch society. The result was a remarkably Balkanized religio-social landscape. One writer describes the socio-religious scene in these somewhat frustrated and ironic terms:

> Historians wishing to record the ecclesiastical history of the country lose heart at the sight of all the church steeples; they trip over many fences and pay their toll at many little religious drawbridges, for in this country where so much water flows, God's water, too, has been canalized and God's acre has been dyked in thoroughly and parceled out minutely.[2]

Family Background

This was the world into which Henri J. M. Nouwen was born, in the Catholic enclave in Nijkerk. His father's family was from the south, from the province of Limburg. His mother was from the more Protestant north. When Henri was born, Catholics made up about 40 percent of the population. His family was described by Peter Naus, a friend from graduate-school days, as "well-educated and rather well-to-do."[3] This is not to say that Henri's family was wealthy; Henri was born in a normal house on a regular, middle-class street. What Naus must have meant is that the Nouwen family had a certain social prominence or respectability as educated people.

When one reads the writings of Henri Nouwen, this background is evident. It is possible to sense not only the high educational standards but also the drive, self-empowerment, and orderliness on which Nouwen drew from this family background. Henri's paternal grandfather had been the town clerk in Venlo, on the German border; Henri's father was a professor of law at the Catholic University of Nijmegen. They were solid, respectable folk with an intellectual bent, moving within the ambit of the smaller cities of the Dutch countryside.

Henri's mother's side of the family was the more prosperous, and also the more artistic and spiritual. His maternal grandmother was left a widow and took over the family business to support her large family. She was successful and became the owner of a local department store. She also seems to have played a special role in the family, and especially in Henri's life, as the guardian or promoter of religious devotion. Her daughter, Henri's mother, Maria, was also very devout. Maria was a cultured woman who not only raised a family but also pursued lively interests in literature and foreign languages. Maria's brother, Henri's uncle Anton, also played an important role in the family circle. As a prominent priest with ecumenical leanings, he was an obvious role model for Henri. This uncle's contacts with Judaism were important ones, and he would become an advisor to the Vatican on Jewish-Christian relations.

A Self-Contained Community

Yet all this was in the future. As a young boy, Henri had virtually no contact with non-Catholics, such was life within the insular Catholic enclave in which he was raised. This was the case for nearly everyone in Holland. Each community, each "column" of Dutch society, not only kept to itself but had numerous markers of community identity. Today, these distinctions have broken down, but vestiges still remain. John Coleman lists a few of the enduring characteristics:

> Anyone, with a few clues and a keen eye, could upon first meeting place a Dutchman in his proper column. Catholics and Protestants wear their wedding rings on different hands. They have separate vocabularies, such as the different ways to refer to "in the first place" when presenting a list of items. First names are often a clue. Old Germanic names such as Dirk, Barend, Aal are most likely non-Catholic. Latinized names such as Titus, Clemens, Aloysius, Cecilia are almost certainly Catholic. The Dutch sign letters or documents with their first two or three initials and the last name. A large proportion of Catholics have M., standing for Maria, for a middle or third initial. The somberness of clothing style, speech, and even facial expression can give away the *Gereformeerde* Dutchmen. Thinking in terms of columnization has become such an ingrained Dutch habit that even opponents of the structure tend to be identified as Catholic,

Protestant, Socialist, or Liberal *"van huis uit"*—in their origins.[4]

This delineation of the different communities explains Nouwen's occasional remarks later in life about growing up in a parochial and sheltered environment. Even as an adult of twenty-five, he reckoned that up to that point he had never in his life met an unbeliever or a divorced person and had had only cautious contacts with Protestants.[5] As Henri went on to become a more and more ecumenical Christian, he often evoked his own simpler origins. By doing so he reminded everyone of how much the world has changed and how many adjustments have been part of the journey for all of us.

Early Signs

Henri was the oldest of his family. He had two younger brothers and a younger sister. Henri was not known in Holland by his given name, but as "Harrie," a more colloquial, northern form of Henri. His talents and abilities were uneven, and this was manifest at an early age. Although an intelligent and restless child, Henri was also clumsy and uncoordinated. He was a natural-born leader, but unable, due to his clumsiness, to excel at sports or games. Perhaps partly for this reason, Henri gravitated very early on to the religious interests and observances that were the underpinnings of his family and their circle. Henri would later tell an interviewer, "Both of my parents are deeply, deeply spiritual people and even my grandmother was even more a person who nurtured my spiritual life. So, when I was five years old, I wanted to be a priest already. I actually never changed my mind. I had that desire from very, very young."[6]

Given how his life would turn out, it seems almost un-canny that even Henri's childhood fantasies and playacting centered around the priesthood. By the time he was eight he had taken on and involved the whole family in a "boy priest" fantasy. As part of this fantasy he convinced them to let him set up a miniature chapel in the attic. There he would dress in liturgical robes made for him by his grandmother's seamstress and say Mass with a paten, chalice, and other liturgical acces-sories also supplied by her. It was his own church, from which he would address "sermons" to the family. His brother Paul was often his attendant, but the whole family and a number of friends could be enlisted in the hierarchy he created.[7]

While eight-year-old Henri was saying Mass in the family attic, the war came to Holland in the form of the German oc-cupation, work camps, and the hunting down of Jews and any-one else who qualified as an enemy of the Third Reich. The Nouwen family did their best to keep a low profile. Henri's mother spoke German fairly well and was able to avoid trouble with the occupying German military. Henri's father needed to stay out of sight to avoid being sent off to a labor camp. He created a hiding place inside a wall where he spent long days and weeks, and on the day German soldiers arrived to search the house, they failed to find him. What we can see from this story is that Henri Nouwen had very capable parents who were able to survive and provide a safe environment for the children, even during the difficult war years.

Schooling for Henri and his younger siblings during most of the war years took place in a makeshift academy begun by the Crozier Fathers in a neighboring village at his mother's urging. Henri's mother was evidently as caring as she was re-sourceful. In all his long life, no person ever mattered to Henri as much as his mother. Henri had a special bond with her, and within the family circle these two especially seemed always to be on the same wavelength. Maria Nouwen was sensitive and thoughtful, and Henri took after her in this regard.

Henri's feelings about his father were more ambivalent. In speaking about him, both Henri and his siblings have used the word "ambitious"[8] to describe his energetic personality. A man of enormous drive and great expectations, Laurent Nouwen was also a hard act for a son to follow. Laurent Nouwen saw himself as a self-made man, and he placed a high value on personal independence. He had made a way for himself in the world and he urged his sons to make something of themselves, also. While Henri was very fortunate to have such an energetic and intelligent father, Henri's own inner uncertainties became tangled, very early on in life, with a sense that he could never measure up to his father's expectations. Part of this may have been due to Henri's own psychology, but not all. Henri's brother, Paul, closest to him in age, thinks that both he, and especially Henri, developed an inferiority complex due to a perceived inability to measure up to the standards of their dynamic father.[9]

Restless and Eager to Begin

By the time he was twelve years old, Henri Nouwen was convinced he wanted to enter the minor seminary, even if this meant living apart from his family. Although sending a boy with a vocation to such a church school was common practice among Catholics at that time, in Nouwen's case his family hesitated. They were ultimately unwilling to commit him to the ecclesiastical path at such a young age. One factor was the war, which by 1944 had reached a critical phase. The Allies had entered France and were moving toward Berlin. Holland would soon be liberated, but fighting was fierce. In view of the volatile state that all the world was in, Henri was kept near home for the time being and enrolled in the local "gymnasium," which is the equivalent to a prep school in German- and Dutch-speaking Europe.

After the war ended, the Nouwens moved to the Hague, the seat of government and the Dutch Parliament, and there Henri finished his secondary education in a Jesuit school, Aloysius College. He then entered the minor seminary at the age of eighteen, there joining other boys of his age who were completing their final year of studies. Henri's uncle Anton—now a monsignor—was head of the same minor seminary, so Henri remained within the family orbit even after becoming a seminarian.

Henri spent a year under Anton's tutelage in the minor seminary, and then moved on to the major seminary. Although one might suppose that he would have been at a disadvantage, socially speaking, by joining the seminary-bound students long after the other boys had sorted themselves into a hierarchy and had achieved cohesion as a group, he made a very favorable impression at the two seminaries and even emerged as a leader. A younger student notes:

> He was the nephew of the minor seminary president so had a kind of aura which was both social and charismatic. All the students liked and admired him so he was elected as senior of the community, which meant that he was a representative in front of the professors and, when the bishop came, he was the speaker. Effectively, he was the head boy.[10]

It is not surprising that Henri was popular with his peers at school. He was pious, hard working, and extremely likable. Finding himself in the minor seminary, it must have seemed to Henri Nouwen that life was finally moving in the direction he wished to go. The war and its immediate aftermath were fading and he had embarked on the path to becoming a priest, the vocation to which he had felt called since childhood. Although he was clearly excelling in his studies, he did not believe later that this was due to any special aptitude or intelligence. Instead, he claimed that it had happened simply because he "worked so crazy hard."[11]

Henri Nouwen entered the minor seminary in 1950, and this bit of chronology is extremely significant in itself. There are occasionally periods of major change in Catholicism, and, due to the fortunes of time and place, Henri Nouwen was to find himself at the epicenter of one of the greatest shifts that the Church has ever made in all its long history. The Catholicism of his youth would be transformed into a very different religion by the time he reached adulthood, and quiet little Holland would play a major role in that transformation.

The Dutch Church

As we have seen, Catholics had for hundreds of years made up an identifiable segment within society in Holland. In part because Holland was a nominally Protestant country, they also insulated themselves in almost ghetto-like fashion from the larger non-Catholic world. The Catholic Dutch were a quiet, worshipful church. Both Pius XI and Pius XII had held up obedient Dutch Catholics as a model for other countries. Indeed, the Catholicism of Nouwen's youth in the Netherlands was in almost obsessive conformity with the official policies of the Vatican.

The Vatican in this period was very much bound up in a centuries-old conflict. Catholicism throughout Europe and the world had been severely challenged by a series of enormous changes in society that had begun in the sixteenth century with the Reformation. First, Protestant churches had come to control the northern countries of Europe. Then the monarchies had fallen in France and Italy and the Church had been stripped of most of its lands and privileges in those countries, too. Finally, in Eastern Europe, in Spain, and in Mexico, socialist governments had arisen and unleashed persecutions on both Orthodox and Catholic churches. The Church was left reeling from these massive and successive assaults on its medieval preeminence. As an institution it seemed to be crumbling.

The Catholic Church's response to this series of challenges and changes was to assume a fortress-like defensive posture and mentality. In a forceful regrouping, the popes from Pius IX in the nineteenth century to Pius XII in the middle of the twentieth century demanded of all Catholics a new level of adherence. A revised and more thoroughgoing code of canon law was issued. Faithful obedience to Vatican directives as well as a careful delineation of all things Catholic from the rest of society were required. All ideas and teachings that were not Catholic in origin came to be regarded as suspect, and even within Catholicism the strictest of measures were taken to ensure complete orthodoxy.

To our eyes today it may seem as if embattled Catholicism went through an especially controlling, paranoid phase of its existence at this time. No priest could publish an article without permission. No theological or spiritual book could be published without ecclesiastical authorization. All seminary lectures were approved by Rome itself. Excommunications occurred without the person censured being present or granted a hearing. The normative spirituality promoted by the Church was a self-denying, otherworldly variety exemplified by Thomas à Kempis's *The Imitation of Christ*. Popes, bishops, and even priests were considered to be part of the supernatural order, thus set off and removed from the natural realm of the laity. This type of Catholicism has been called triumphalist, and rightly so. Its attitude to the modern world and other religions was dismissive.

Catholics in the Netherlands accepted this system without question. There was an even greater degree of triumphal separatism in the Catholic community in Holland than elsewhere. Dutch Catholicism was highly organized and monolithic, even in comparison to Catholic communities in neighboring countries. Ninety percent of Catholic youngsters attended Catholic elementary schools. Eighty-nine percent of the Catholic population had paid subscriptions to the Catholic radio company. Seventy-nine percent read Catholic daily newspapers. Seventy-five percent attended weekly Mass.[12] The Dutch Church was the most faithful and traditional in Europe, the most opposed to ecumenism, and the highest per capita contributor of missionary priests, nuns, and religious workers to the Church. The Dutch comprised 10 percent of all missionary personnel worldwide.[13]

As a Dutch Catholic with a call to the priesthood in the 1950s, Henri Nouwen was therefore raised within a benevolent but authoritarian parochial culture with very clear boundaries. Loyalty and obedience to the Vatican were instilled in Catholics from infancy, and anyone unable to adhere to the rules was subject to both social and religious censure. Nouwen recalls that the greatest scandal of his youth occurred when a friend of his left the seminary.[14] In today's twenty-first-century world, many regard Islam as a religion of narrow-mindedness and submission, but we sometimes forget that a mere fifty or sixty years ago, Roman Catholicism insisted on the strictest adherence to an all-embracing system of law, liturgy, education, marriage, and social and political expression, particularly in countries like Holland.

Henri Nouwen was very much a part of this religious and cultural dynamic. This does not mean that he had no freedom. His life may have been protected, but it was far from cloistered. He was allowed to visit with and travel with his family. However, like seminary students everywhere, Nouwen lived a fairly regimented life in the seminary and had little unstructured time. He passed his days studying, attending Mass, and participating in visits, charity work, and other church activities, all the while preparing to take his vows, by which he would give up his own personal autonomy in order to serve God and serve his bishop. Taking this final step was not a difficult decision for Henri. Despite his father's belief in the importance of independence, the culture in which Henri had grown up was based on daily choices to be a practicing Catholic. The columnized arrangement of Dutch society made such choices clearer and easier, and Dutch society was naturally conservative and even conformist.

When we think of Henri today, we must remember that his beginnings were in this different world, one that created among the faithful a spiritual certainty that we have since lost almost completely. I remember recounting the story of my own youth to Henri one night over dinner. We were in Cambridge, Massachusetts, and his sister Laurien was visiting him at the time. I had grown up in California during the more turbulent 1960s, and Henri's first reaction on hearing the story of my youth was one of wide-eyed astonishment at how "rebellious" it all seemed compared to his own! Indeed, Henri's early life was part of a different age.

If Catholic belief was regimented and did not allow for much doubt or individual expression, the result was not mere authoritarianism. At that time and in those circles there flourished a culture that honored purity, discipline, and self-sacrifice. Moreover, Catholics of that era knew how to articulate and pass on clearly stated values to their children and to the rest of the world. In Holland especially, Catholics were confident, self-assured, and disciplined.

The Birth of a New Catholicism

However, a change was coming. Already in the 1950s, when Henri Nouwen was studying for the priesthood, fissures and cracks had begun to appear in the façade of the Roman Catholic edifice. There had, of course, been real flaws in the Catholicism of Nouwen's youth, especially in terms of its relationship with the larger world. The Church was overly authoritarian, gripped by a paralyzing fear of socialism, unresponsive to its members' needs, and deeply mistrustful of the modern world.

For that reason, within the Church there were initiatives being made toward renewal and the updating of the Church's theology. World War II had disrupted the Church's routines. During the war, the Germans had put many Catholic priests from occupied countries to work as laborers. In France especially, this led to a desire on the part of the clergy to continue sharing in the life of working people on a voluntary basis after hostilities ceased. Many priests took jobs in factories and even became members of labor unions. Theologians in France meanwhile also experimented with other means to engage the world and to make sense of the scientific advances and social changes that had occurred in the twentieth century.

The response of Pius XII to these new initiatives and experiments in France and elsewhere was negative and authoritarian. In 1950 the pope issued an encyclical, *Humani Generis*, forbidding progressive initiatives within Catholicism. The priest-worker movement was curtailed. The leading theologians involved with the new currents were transferred and silenced. Officially, the traditional approach was reaffirmed.

However, the new ideas did not disappear. They gathered strength quietly, and from France they easily spread to neighboring Belgium and Holland. Throughout the 1950s, the years when Nouwen was a seminarian, a groundswell of new thinking swept the Dutch Church, and in Holland, unlike most other countries, many of the bishops and clergy allowed and encouraged this process. Henri himself found a special entrée into this new world through his uncle, who was involved in ecumenical outreach to both Protestants and Jews. As the new ideas circulated, as new connections outside Catholicism became possible, Henri was not only learning and observing, but occasionally in fact participating in new ways of being a Dutch Catholic.

One reason why the Dutch bishops were more open or less authoritarian than bishops elsewhere was their unique experience during the war. Although the Catholic Church in most European countries had done little to oppose the Nazis, the Dutch bishops had shown great courage and mounted actual resistance. They had urged non-cooperation with the Nazis and protested every German misdeed, including the persecution and removal of the Jews. The Catholic University of Nijmegen was closed over the Catholic refusal to take loyalty oaths, and many Dutch Catholics were harassed, punished, and sent to work camps and even concentration camps.

These hardships resulted in the fostering of an unusual solidarity and loyalty between the Dutch laity and their bishops. It was a solidarity that was to continue once the war ended. The war also brought down the wall between Dutch Catholics and Protestants. As Frederick Franck puts it:

> [T]he occupation disturbed the idyll. The cozy but militant group-togethernesses of the denominations ended suddenly, and the army, the prisons and concentration camps threw together people who suddenly discovered all that they had in common...Together they

learned what tyranny, terrorism and dictatorship meant
in practice...After the war nothing that even reminds
one of this tutelage and despotism is tolerated.[15]

Put simply, after the war the old style of benevolent religious
authoritarianism could not continue. During the 1950s, new
social attitudes appeared and flourished among the Dutch. The
columnization of society started to break down. The demo-
cratic impulses of an educated populace took hold within the
ecclesiastical realm. A new kind of Catholicism open to the
laity began to emerge. Consultation and collaboration became
the norm in ecclesiastical affairs. Although such open demo-
cratic practices contradicted the top-down policies of official
Catholicism, they seemed increasingly natural and normal in
the Dutch context.

What was Nouwen's participation in the new Catholicism?
He was first a seminarian, then a newly ordained priest when
these changes began to take place. Being a young person, he
had no commitments to the older observances, yet he still had
a great deal to unlearn. The pious practices of previous decades
—and previous centuries—were being scrutinized by those
around him and often discarded. The Church was attempting
to speak to the needs of modern people in a changing world.
Many of the devotions of Nouwen's youth were subsumed and
lost as the Church shifted to a more biblical and psychologically sensitive spirituality. Most important, the Church tried to
become more inclusive and attentive to its members. These
were changes that Nouwen accepted and internalized. They
would become hallmarks of the spirituality he would teach and
promote for the rest of his life.

We have a portrait of Nouwen's style as it emerged in the
fifties, one drawn by Peter Naus, whose fiancée took instruction in Catholicism from Henri. He remembers Henri this
way:

The three of us met for almost a year in 1958, and our sessions had a lasting impact on me. Henri paid little attention to church dogma or to rules and conventions. Instead, he made the teachings of Christ his focus. I was forced to reexamine my own faith, which was the product of a highly conservative religious upbringing. I challenged Henri many times when I thought there was a contradiction between what I had been taught to believe and what he propagated. Gently and patiently he loosened my rigid and unyielding faith stance and helped me shift from a preoccupation with external practices based on dogmatic beliefs to the exploration of a personal connection with Christ. While our sessions were meant to guide Anke's conversion, in many ways they brought about my own conversion as well.

I am rather certain that Henri's instruction was different from [the type of instruction] current at the time. He was more daring, less conventional, more pastoral than other priests I knew. That has always surprised me, especially when I discovered his almost scrupulous fear of deviating from church teaching and altering church rituals, though this fear abated in later years.[16]

Several things are noteworthy in Naus's account of young Henri Nouwen's pastoral style. For one thing, we see that he was clearly imbued with the new theological thinking. In fact, he seems to have grasped its true import, which was to create a more authentic spirituality with Jesus at the center, not merely to make changes in the Church's style at an institutional level. Also worth noting is the "almost scrupulous fear" that Naus mentions. Nouwen went beyond the bounds of orthodox expression, yet it was never his intention to be rebellious. This apparent paradox would continue to be an issue for most of his life. In the end, Nouwen burst the bounds of Christian tradition and moved to a new level without acknowledging that he had done so. But that lay in the future. In his early years in Holland he was moving forward with new formulations and new ideas, but only as part of a national movement involving the majority of his peers, his teachers, and even his bishops. He was in step, not out of step, with those around him.

As Dutch Catholicism became increasingly committed to exploration and dialogue, exchanges continued between theologians, lay experts representing numerous fields, and the bishops. Beginning in the university, then elsewhere, liturgical experiments had also begun to take place. Many of the hallmarks of the modern Catholic liturgy, including the use of the vernacular in the liturgy, reception of communion in the hand, and the use of lay ministers and readers in the service, began as experiments in Holland. At one point the novelties became so noticeable and newsworthy that travel agents in France promoted tours of the Netherlands not to see the tulips, but "the new Catholicism!"

What happened in Holland in the late fifties and early sixties was something like a theological "Prague Spring." Excitement was everywhere and for most Dutch Catholics it was a thrilling time of tremendous optimism. Everyone was in dialogue with everyone. Nouwen was part of this experience. He had found his voice as a communicative preacher and began publishing articles. In church circles he was recognized as a bright young man with a future. He had already proved himself to be a diligent student and a gifted speaker, so the chancery offered him the chance to continue his theological education in Rome. After receiving further training there, he would then return to teach in the seminary or elsewhere and continue to be a model for younger priests.

Nouwen's bishop was Archbishop Bernard Alfrink, a biblical scholar and former professor at the University of Nijmegen.

He transferred to the episcopal chancery in 1951 and became archbishop of Utrecht in 1955. Despite his later reputation as a progressive, Alfrink did not begin his episcopal career as a convinced liberal, as can be seen from his early pronouncements. Rather, Alfrink was an open-minded man who became a full participant in the extraordinary dialogue that began in Holland at this time. Being part of the Dutch experience and taking part in the extraordinary dialogue changed his attitudes and made him a special kind of bishop. He proved to have a particular genius for engagement. He not only worked closely with the other bishops but set up structures, such as a national pastoral council, to foster new levels of shared responsibility and dialogue throughout the Church.

Alfrink would become internationally famous for championing progressive forms of Catholicism at Vatican II. He was extremely effective at the council in Rome. This effectiveness came about in part because the Dutch episcopacy and Church were behind him, and in part because of the expert help he relied on, especially that of theologian Edward Schillebeeckx. Fr. Schillebeeckx had come to Holland as an agent of change. As a Belgian and a French speaker, he had been part of the new theology emerging in France. When he was named to a chair in Nijmegen, he brought to the university a new model of inquiry and of engagement with the social sciences, psychology, and phenomenology. Because theology within Dutch universities had previously had little input from other disciplines, Schillebeeckx caused a great stir.[17]

Turning in a New Direction

It was a time of new possibilities. Nouwen considered the offer to continue his studies in Rome and made a counterproposal— he wanted to continue studying, but not in Rome. Instead, he wanted to work in one of the exciting new disciplines that Catholics were just then discovering. He asked for permission to enter the doctoral program in psychology at Nijmegen. This proposal was accepted and he joined the student body in the same year that Schillebeeckx joined the faculty, 1957.

Nouwen would attend Nijmegen University for seven years, there learning the fundamentals of clinical psychology. Pathologies, research samples, statistics, schemas of personality development, and case studies now formed important new fields of reference for him. Although psychological theory in Holland and in Europe generally was becoming more and more influenced by American developments, it was still heavily freighted with continental philosophical thinking and with the spirit of Freud and Jung.[18] Freud had died during the war, but Jung was still alive. In the intellectual ambiance of university life throughout Europe, the ideas of both these seminal figures reverberated and found new adherents. Both had a profound impact, not only on their own discipline, but on the broader culture. Theories of an unconscious self, of the inalienable sexuality of human beings, of multiple centers of personality— such as the ego, the superego and the id—and many other progressive and unsettling ideas were in the air.

Nouwen's entry into Nijmegen University at the age of twenty-five thus signaled the end of the relatively simple uniformity of his youth. Not only was he facing new ideas and challenges as a graduate student, but he was drawn into the activities and endless discussions of university life. Here was an opportunity to be part of an interesting new environment and, even more important, to both live and promote the emerging Dutch Catholicism in a public arena. With his solid belief system and extroverted personality, Henri Nouwen was magnetically drawn into campus conversation and debate. As Michael Ford writes:

Throughout his time at Nijmegen Nouwen stood out for his enthusiasm and intensity. With his theological education and the blessing of the Church, he seems to have been active in all kinds of meetings for students who were amazed by his proclivity to talk. Although it was a Catholic university, many students tended to be anticlerical and Nouwen clearly had a rough ride at times, though he won many friends and admirers, too.[19]

Meanwhile, in his formal studies Nouwen was encountering greater difficulty. Although there was a religious component to the department (Han Fortmann, a leading figure investigating the psychological interplay of religion and culture, was there and had a great impact on Henri), the philosophical underpinnings of psychology were starkly different from the theological outlook Nouwen had absorbed in his formative training.

Freud, for example, cast doubt on such well-established, even classical concepts as virtue, civilization, and belief in God and providence. According to Freud, all human motivations stem from conflicts and experiences in our infancy which are buried in our unconscious so that we can cope with life and progress into adulthood. All behavior ultimately derives from primitive drives—either a libidinal or "sex" drive and an aggressive or "death" drive. For Freud, even great moral or intellectual achievements are motivated by these shadowy, primitive urges. His view of human nature was empirical and deterministic. In Freud's view, everyone is pathological at some level, given the inevitable conflicts that occur during psychosexual development.

Religion was treated by Freud as both an illusion and a neurosis. When we face the terrors of life in the real world as children, we fabricate for ourselves a benevolent deity modeled on our expectations and our experiences of our fathers. None of Freud's theories is easily reconciled with Christian thinking.[20] With some justification, believing Christians and Jews alike regarded Freud, the father of modern psychoanalysis, with concern and even alarm.[21] One can just imagine young Henri Nouwen's shock upon learning what Freud actually thought.

Nor was Freud the only challenging new voice. Carl Jung's approach initially seemed more palatable, but it recast and altered concepts that were long a part of Christian ideology. The Jungian worldview, like the Chinese concept of yin and yang, is based on binary opposition—if there is human consciousness, then there is also human unconsciousness. If one is consciously male, then one is also latently or unconsciously female—this is the famous *animus* or *anima*. In this tension between opposites, if any phenomenon appears, its opposite is suppressed or left undeveloped.

Undeveloped characteristics do not merely remain absent. They lie in hidden recesses within the human psyche. They are like clothing one owns but never wears. From these recesses, our undeveloped sides exert hidden pressure on our psyches. The "shadow" is like a psychic limbo of unchosen and undeveloped personal options carried within. Jung was convinced that earlier ages and more primitive people had greater access to the unconscious than do modern people. His works are filled with brilliant though rambling analyses of ancient, medieval, or aboriginal images, myths, and practices used to explain the fundamentals of the soul. Jungian psychoanalysis is an exploration of one's inner landscape and its archetypes, leading not only to health but also to individuation and an encounter with one's higher self, which some people may wish to call God.[22]

Jung was a pessimist with regard to theology. He believed that psychological projections so cloud our view of the deity as to make true knowledge of God a virtual impossibility. Jung's treatment of religion was forever two-sided. As the traumatized son of an equally traumatized Protestant minister, Jung bore a considerable grudge against Christianity. However, he accepted Christian rituals and beliefs, particularly those of medieval Catholicism, as both interesting and psychologically meaningful and beneficial. His premises and methods appealed to many Christians and Jung found himself surrounded by religious people and even scholars who became devoted to his cause. He himself vacillated between positive and negative estimations of the value and truth of religion.[23]

Freud and Jung have now been absorbed and assimilated and are part of the common culture of the West. However, this brief sketch of their basic ideas perhaps conveys some sense of the profoundly challenging, even disturbing ideologies that Henri Nouwen confronted as a young graduate student in psychology. As a priest who was directly engaged in the controversial new "science of the mind," Henri Nouwen could be counted a bold pioneer in the 1950s and 1960s. No immediate synthesis was possible between the quite divergent value systems of Catholicism and psychological theory when Nouwen was a student, so he spent years commuting mentally between two very different views of reality. Both of these mutually exclusive thought worlds demanded a high level of allegiance from Henri. Thus, he must have faced innumerable conflicts in fulfilling his obligations as both a graduate student and a priest.

Serious difficulties also began to arise regarding his program. Henri Nouwen was surely capable of absorbing the vocabulary, the methodology, and the underlying theories of psychology and philosophy during his first years of study. However, once he knew enough about clinical psychology to form an independent personal judgment, he must have realized he was in the wrong program, or even the wrong field entirely. Clinical psychology attempts to bring scientific rigor to the study of human nature. It is also often reductive, dependent on testing and statistical models, and can seem coldly uncaring in its analysis of pathologies and clinical conditions. None of this was of much interest to Henri Nouwen. Able to complete a case study, Nouwen was nevertheless temperamentally unsuited to serious independent psychological research, which requires months or years of solitary study and immersion in sometimes numbingly dry fields of data. Never one for abstraction or detailed minutiae, Nouwen must have felt he had hit a solid wall that he could not climb as he put in year after year in pursuit of a doctorate in clinical psychology.

Another basic problem was the lack of integration. Today, anyone entering a fully stocked bookstore will find the psychology section right alongside the religion section and there will be numerous titles which could be cross-filed under both headings. However, it has taken half a century to achieve such a rapprochement between the two fields. The situation in the Netherlands when Nouwen was in graduate school was hardly multidisciplinary.

The First Great Test

So, what began as an intellectual challenge and an opportunity to engage in the vanguard of an experimental discipline began to sour for Nouwen. This program was not one in which he could ultimately succeed, and he began to ask himself and others whether he should even complete the degree. Entering this program appears to have been a wrong turn, one that was not necessarily Nouwen's fault. Once beyond the initial steps and requirements, success in academia depends on many uncontrollable variables. One commits to a long program of study or a research project without knowing if it will lead in the right direction or fit one personally. In Nouwen's case, it was a poor fit indeed.

Perhaps there is a spiritual lesson here regarding how God guides his people. Although we all remember the story of the Israelites wandering in the wilderness, we cling to the belief that people who have found God's favor should exhibit both certainty and clear direction. We think they should fly as straight as arrows. However, this is frequently not the case. As we examine the lives of the saints, beginning with Jacob, the biblical patriarch who worked seven years to marry the wrong woman,[24] we see how often mistakes are made, time is lost, and detours are taken. In this regard, Nouwen was like many who had gone before him. His doctoral studies were not turning out as he had expected. He was not a success at everything, and, in this case, he was not to become a normal or typical academic.

Perhaps there was another, less clearly defined conflict that was part of Nouwen's growing discomfort with his psychological training. To become a psychological or medical professional involves taking on the serious demeanor and detachment that we all expect from someone with scientific training. Nouwen was undergoing a type of schooling that in our culture amounts to an initiation. He was supposed to emerge on the other side of graduate school as a medical professional, ready to adhere to the standards of practice relevant to that discipline.

Henri Nouwen became less and less willing to endorse or participate in this socialization and personal packaging as his years of training proceeded. Each step he took toward becoming a psychologist may have seemed to be taking him farther and farther away from the ideals of the gospel. There were also aspects of his own psychology that made it doubly hard for him to take on the trappings of professionalism.

I will deal with this issue further in the next chapter on Nouwen's psychology, but here I will say that Henri resisted growing completely into adulthood. He had a playful, childlike disposition. This was the source of his artistic awareness, his innocent creativity, and his automatic identification with children and young people. He was what Carl Jung and his follow-ers call a *puer aeternus*, a person who remains childlike in adult-hood. While he was a seminarian, his charming *puer* attitude was perfectly acceptable, but the pressured socialization he faced in graduate school was a challenge that few *puer* types could have endured.

For all these reasons Nouwen began to reject the model of the psychologist-doctor. He never became a "professional" person, the equivalent to his professorial father. He took a dif-ferent path, and the discomfort he felt about professionalism was to last and become part of who he was. It is not an accident that his first independent book, *Creative Ministry*, included criticism of the professional attitudes taken by ministers.[25] This rejection of the professional model would continue as a theme running through his life and teaching. An example of Nouwen's anti-professionalism can even be found in one of his last books, *In the Name of Jesus*, where he wrote:

> As Jesus ministers, so he wants us to minister. He wants Peter to feed his sheep and care for them, not as "pro-fessionals" who know their clients' problems and take care of them, but as vulnerable brothers and sisters who know and are known, who care and are cared for, who forgive and are being forgiven, who love and are being loved. Somehow we have come to believe that good leadership requires a safe distance from those we are called to lead. Medicine, psychiatry, and social work all offer us models in which "service" takes place in a one-way direction. Someone serves, someone else is being served, and be sure not to mix up the roles! . . . The world in which we live—a world of efficiency and control— has no models to offer to those who want to be shep-herds in the way Jesus was a shepherd.[26]

This anti-professional attitude began to crystallize during Nouwen's graduate student years. He would come to regard the philosophy of professionalism more and more as something profoundly dehumanizing and simply unchristian.

Thus it was that Henri Nouwen began to consider alternatives to his program. While in this "escape mode" he took an unpaid position as chaplain on the Holland-America cruise line, and this made possible some travel to the United States, a country that was beckoning him for several reasons. For one thing, by the early sixties, the United States was becoming a leader in the field of psychology. Nouwen knew that there were programs in the United States that combined psychology and religion in a hybrid discipline called "pastoral counseling." While on a stopover in Boston, he wrangled an invitation to speak with a Harvard psychologist, Gordon Allport, who was known to be sympathetic to the new combined discipline. Allport told Nouwen that he should finish his degree and then go to the Menninger Foundation in Kansas if he wanted to pursue the interdisciplinary approach. The choice of the Menninger Foundation would later be confirmed for Nouwen through another contact, Seward Hiltner of Princeton, to whom Nouwen wrote in 1964. During the 1960s, a number of the leading figures involved in the growing interplay of psychiatry and psychology with religion and the social sciences were gathered at the Menninger facility.

Defining His Own Agenda

Nouwen's conversation with Gordon Allport at Harvard made it clear he would have to stick it out in Holland and finish his thesis. However, Nouwen's choice of a thesis topic could not have been more indicative of the direction in which he was leaning. He chose to examine the work of Anton Boisen, the American minister credited with being the originator of clinical pastoral education in U.S. seminaries. Although Boisen had made an important contribution to society, his personal struggles had also made him a tragic figure.

Boisen was born in Indiana in 1876. The family milieu in which he grew up was academic and religious, much like Henri's own. Boisen worked in two fields. He was a pastor and also did work in forestry science. However, he suffered a mental breakdown and was interned in a mental hospital for a fifteen-month period. From within that locked ward, Boisen began to interpret his plunge into mental illness as a call to repentance and self-examination. He actively fought his way up from depression and psychosis and back to health. In the process, he realized that his experiences, his friends and his loved ones, even his education, were the basis of his recovery. In traversing the fine line between psychosis and mental health, what had mattered most was his own previous life experience, those whom he cared for, and God. He also rigorously examined his "background" to find some explanation for his mysterious mental illness. When he was released and looked back on the whole process, he realized that what had happened to him was akin to a religious call. His hospitalization, far from representing an interruption of his career, became the foundation of everything he did from then on.

He enrolled himself in Andover Theological Seminary in Massachusetts and at the same time began taking classes at Harvard. There he met Richard Cabot, M.D., scion of an aristocratic Boston family and the man credited with adapting the case study method, then used at Harvard Law School, to medicine. In the conversations that took place between Boisen and Cabot at Harvard, they came to further realizations. The case study idea made plain what Boisen had discovered in overcoming his own illness: real-life situations, especially those one experiences personally, are more valuable than any abstract text-book approach to learning.

Later, Boisen was appointed chaplain of Worcester State Hospital, one of the main psychiatric hospitals in Massachu-setts. There he was able to implement his theories, inviting theological students to share in the care of sick people, making ministers part of therapeutic alliances with doctors and nurses, and promoting clinical pastoral education in seminaries across the country. Throughout his career, he continued to regard his own life and thought process as a primary source of truth and inspiration. His mental health was never totally assured—his colleagues and students sometimes had doubts about his men-tal competence. In his own mind there was a link between reli-gious experience and mental illness, and he did not strive to be other than he was. He was a tragic figure, a creative genius and a wounded healer whose mine of insights was his own suffer-ing, much like Vincent van Gogh, and much like Henri Nouwen himself would become later in life.[27]

Nouwen's thesis on Boisen, when presented in Nijmegen University, was not immediately approved. Henri was told that if it were to be accepted, he would have to recast the thesis as a more scientific work based on statistics and clinical models. Henri balked at this attempt to "straitjacket" him into a narrow professionalism.[28] He determined to drop the ill-fated thesis and leave Nijmegen with a *doctorandus* degree. The *doctorandus* in Holland is a professional qualification, while the doctorate is an academic, research degree.[29]

Vatican II

At the same time that Henri Nouwen was working to finish his thesis and then seeing it rejected by the psychology faculty of Nijmegen University, much was happening in the Church.

Bernard Alfrink, who had been made a cardinal in 1960, was appointed to the commission that was to organize and prepare for the Second Vatican Council. This historic consultation was called by John XXIII, whose papacy was devoted to ending the years of triumphalism and moving the Church out of its medieval mindset and beyond the paranoid policies of previous centuries. Once the council began, the French theological style and spirit quickly won out over a more traditional Germanic approach, and many of the currents repressed during the previous twenty years came bursting back to the surface.

The council began officially in 1962. The Dutch, although a numerical minority, played a critical role at the council because of their ability to work as a team and their formidable media apparatus. The state-subsidized Dutch information center, Documentazione Olandese del Concilio (DOC), was able, on short notice, to produce learned background reports drawn up by progressive theologians and translated into all the major languages. These documents often became the basis for conciliar discussions. Journalists attending the council, usually unable to access Vatican representatives, came to regard the DOC as a briefing room disseminating the latest news on conciliar developments. Thus, there was strong Dutch influence in both the organization of the council and in the issuing of conciliar news and decisions. It was at the Vatican Council that the Catholic world became clearly aware of the advancing state of Dutch theology. Many of the proposed changes in ecclesiastical structure and in the liturgy were already taking place on an experimental basis in Holland. Cardinal Alfrink, along with Belgium's Cardinal Suenens, emerged as the leaders of the progressive bishops present and working in Rome.

Henri Nouwen was in Rome at various points during the council, and anyone familiar with his books and with Catholic theology can easily recognize the great influence that Vatican II had on him. This council moved the Church's focus from received, or late medieval, tradition back to the Bible and the early Church. It refocused on Christ, rather than the saints. The Church and the Church's apostolate were redefined to include the laity. It was further recognized that the Catholic Church had no monopoly on truth or on salvation. Orthodox and Protestant observers were present at the council, and many of the theological insights of both Christian groups were recognized and incorporated into the conciliar documents. All persons were recognized as having personal religious freedom and freedom of conscience.

In essence, Vatican II sought to update and clarify the Church's theology vis-à-vis the modern world, other religions, and the laity. The Church recognized positive values and much merit in each of these previously neglected areas. Vatican II also sought to produce a more humble, biblical, and open-minded Catholic priesthood and hierarchy. Where once there had been separation and superiority, Vatican II sought to bring openness and a more unassuming spirit.

Henri Nouwen's arrival in United States in 1964 for studies at the Menninger Foundation coincided with the third session of the council. It was at this time that the council promulgated the Dogmatic Constitution on the Church, the Decree on Ecumenism, and the Decree on the Eastern Catholic Churches. The developments in Rome may have been revolutionary for many, but they must have seemed perfectly natural to Henri Nouwen, who had been living a Vatican II–style spirituality for years. After all, his bishop was Cardinal Alfrink himself, and many of the changes proposed in Rome had had their origins in France, Belgium, or Holland. As a Dutch priest who had been in Rome during conciliar sessions, Henri Nouwen was regarded in Kansas as a living representative of the new Catholicism among the Americans he met there. Although his primary focus continued to be the application of psychological theory to pastoral ministry, he quickly found a new role or "vocation" as a proponent of Vatican II spirituality in the United States.

Menninger and Notre Dame

Nouwen's experience at the Menninger Foundation was one he was to remember for the rest of his life as a time of real learning. Karl Menninger was an example of the kind of doctor that Henri Nouwen might have hoped to be. Besides being known for his purely clinical work in psychiatry, Menninger was a public figure who had a great deal to say about American society, its values, and its needs. Many practitioners of the interdisciplinary pastoral psychology that Nouwen wished to investigate were attached to the Foundation.

In Kansas Nouwen was finally able to connect to the world he had glimpsed through Boisen's writings—a world where religion and psychology could be combined and the human dimension was not lost from view. One important contact he made there was with John Dos Santos, a director of research programs. Nouwen and Dos Santos both participated in a small discussion group of Catholics active in the Foundation. Dos Santos was to become not only a good friend, but a key to Henri's immediate future. In a remembrance of Nouwen he tells the story of how this happened:

> Shortly after I went to the University of Notre Dame in 1965 to establish the Department of Psychology and its graduate program, I asked Henri if he would be interested in coming to South Bend as a faculty member. He agreed but expressed some concern about his lack of academic experience and the challenges for him of working in an American institution. My decision to invite Henri into the department was based on his differ-

ent educational and cultural background and his promise as a mentor, counselor, and teacher. I also thought
that I could trust him to be an honest and realistic ad-
viser as I developed a psychology program in a Roman
Catholic university that was still not entirely comfortable with the discipline.

Indeed, about such issues Henri proved to be quite
open-minded and practical. But he tended to be much
more reticent about strictly academic and departmen-
tal matters. From its inception the department was
strongly oriented toward scientific psychology and research. I suspect that this emphasis made Henri feel
somewhat marginal and uncomfortable. He wanted to
be better informed about our research on perception
and cognition, so another faculty member and I discussed conceptualization, research design and methodology, statistical analysis of results, and hypothesis
testing with him. He was very interested and attentive
but quickly realized that this was not the sort of study
he wanted to pursue. Soon afterward he became more
involved with pastoral theology.[30]

From what he has written, it sounds as if John Dos Santos
wanted a priest on his side in facing off with the Notre Dame
administration and he turned to Henri Nouwen for that help.
We can see that even at Notre Dame Nouwen was still struggling with accepting the role of clinician or professional scholar,
the type of individual who usually teaches at large universities.
Clearly intelligent and gifted as a teacher, he was still not interested in or able to do the type of technical research on which
universities and university faculties build their reputations.
Even as Nouwen was becoming better known in American university and church circles, his non-scholarly orientation continued to be a liability. A doctorate was by now considered a

minimum requirement for permanent employment in American academia, and the Notre Dame administration made clear to Nouwen that he had no real future there without fulfilling this requirement.

This seemed to indicate what the next step should be for Nouwen. He had been thinking for years about recasting his Boisen research in terms of pastoral theology. To that end he had been writing about a case study while in the United States. He left Notre Dame, returned to Holland, and began to fulfill the non-thesis requirements for another doctorate in Nijmegen, but this time in theology. While living in Holland and working on his doctorate, he taught in two theological faculties, one in Amsterdam and one in Utrecht.

One Door Closes, Another Opens

This was an unhappy time in Nouwen's life. Back in Holland he felt terribly out of step with the Dutch Church. The Vatican had finally reacted to the Dutch "revolution" in church polity with a firm disavowal.[31] Particularly unpopular in Rome was the idea of a national pastoral council that included laymen and that issued policy recommendations (including some very liberal suggestions such as allowing priests to marry). Having decided that Dutch theology needed to be reined in, the Vatican subsequently began to appoint as new bishops only those Dutch clergyman who were vocally opposed to the new currents in Dutch Catholicism.

The reaction to these Vatican appointments was anger and polarization among the Dutch Catholic laity and a considerable drop in church attendance and involvement. The secularization of society, decried by religious people elsewhere, was hailed as a positive trend by many Catholics in Holland, who interpreted secularization to mean the end of ghetto Catholicism and of the control of society by the Church. Having enjoyed a brief "springtime" of exciting renewal, Dutch Catholicism became fragmented and embittered. The popular priests now were the ones who made manifest this sentiment, the ones who took an active role in opposing the Vatican.

Henri Nouwen's convictions, bolstered by his years of studying Boisen and his experiences in the United States, focused more and more on individual spiritual experience. The institutional struggles taking place in the Dutch Church he found unpalatable, particularly insofar as they involved denouncing bishops or opposing church policy. He became the odd man out. In this regard, it is likely that the coherence of Dutch society worked very much against Henri. The Dutch had reached a consensus, but it had taken place in his absence and he was not part of that consensus. It was a lonely time and he found himself looking away, focusing on his connections in the United States and pursuing publication possibilities there.

When he finally presented his thesis to the theology department at Nijmegen, the result was much the same as it had been in the department of psychology: his thesis was found lacking in theological depth and was rejected in its initial form. Henri thought he would have to begin another thesis on another topic, a commitment that would require a minimum of two or three more years. He was unwilling to make this commitment and decided to drop his bid for a doctorate. He was ultimately issued a second Nijmegen *doctorandus* degree. Only later in his life would he be issued several honorary doctorates in United States.

It is understandable that Henri Nouwen felt great ambivalence at this point about both Holland and the Dutch Church. Not only was his scholarship rejected, but the Catholicism in that country was rapidly changing. Meanwhile, Yale University asked him to come for a visit and surprised him with a job offer when he got there. This he refused, saying his future was in

Holland. However, possibilities in the United States continued to present themselves. Even Yale University renewed its offer. The second time he was asked, Henri accepted. This decision was the real start of his one-man mission to the American continent. Yale thought it was getting a Catholic priest with psychological expertise, but once Henri Nouwen reached Yale and set to work, it became clear that he had decided to leave the psychological approach behind. Some of the technical terms and insights of psychology could still be found in his work for the next decade, but as he began to emerge as a Christian writer with a national reputation, he was clearly working from a spiritual perspective.

A Favored Son

Thus, Henri Nouwen's life in Holland drew to a close. What, then, can be said in summary about Nouwen's Dutch background and the many influences and experiences of his early years? Looking back, particularly to his youth, I regard Henri as living the life of a favored son. As such, he automatically enjoyed a certain status—he was expected by his family to do great things and he was chosen by the Church to provide leadership for the next generation. Perhaps the greatest event of his early years, one he never really acknowledged, was the Second Vatican Council and its prelude. World War II had created the necessary conditions for a complete renewal of theology and spirituality. The leaders of the reform movement were first French, then Belgian and Dutch, and Holland became an experimental laboratory where a new type of Catholic Christianity was tested and developed. It was a time of great freedom and idealism, and Henri Nouwen's own bishop, Cardinal Alfrink, endorsed and promoted change in the Church.

Henri came of age in a time of openness, optimism, and revitalization. Alfrink allowed the young Henri Nouwen the freedom to pursue graduate studies in psychology, first at Nijmegen University, then at the Menninger Foundation. The cardinal even visited Nouwen at the Foundation in Kansas. Henri Nouwen was extremely lucky to have this much support and latitude. While most of his classmates were assigned to normal parish duties, he was allowed to study and roam the world. It was indeed the treatment due a favored son. Decades later, when Nouwen became a public figure in church circles in the United States, he drew on the inclusive, biblical, and Christ-centered teachings of the great Vatican II–era theologians, such as Schillebeeckx. He had absorbed these ideas at such a young age that he did not view them as anything controversial. How could something based on the Bible, approved by the bishops, and taught in the schools be wrong? Thus he continued to embody the early spirit of Vatican II when many Catholics went back to business as usual.

The great obstacle that prevented Henri Nouwen from slipping into a normal life as a college or seminary professor was his inability or unwillingness to engage in serious scholarship. We might be tempted to say that the fault here lay in the fact that Henri Nouwen was ahead of his time. When he entered graduate school, the discipline of pastoral psychology did not really exist. Ironically, today Holland is a leader in the field of pastoral psychology,[32] but in Henri Nouwen's time there were only two options: clinical psychology or the religion and culture studies of someone like Han Fortmann.

Doctoral work at Nijmegen University was the greatest test Henri Nouwen faced as a young man. His two failed bids to win a doctorate were great disappointments. It is interesting that Henri interpreted these episodes as attempts to tie him down and force him to conform. He had a vision for a new approach to the field. Someone without Nouwen's strong sense of self might have simply resigned himself to settling for something from the available menu of possibilities and becoming a seminary professor of psychological studies. However, Nouwen had learned by studying Boisen that adversity and even disaster could be decisive in leading a person into his or her most significant work. This was perhaps what had happened to him, too: if he had been comfortable in clinical psychology and in the Dutch Church, he never would have come to America and found his voice as a prophet here. However, his repeated failures in the field of psychology left their mark. To the end of his life he remained ambivalent about psychology and professionalism in general.

Henri Nouwen ended up working for most of his life in universities, but never again would he attempt the scholarly or intellectual approach. By the time he reached Yale he had claimed his place in academia as a minister. In this we see his individualism and the strength of his call. Yale turned out to be an ideal environment for Henri Nouwen, an environment in which he could flourish. As a European diocesan priest working in a university that was both Protestant and American, he would have unparalleled freedom to teach and to minister as he saw fit. Also, because Yale was a Protestant school, Henri not only was able but was virtually compelled to take Catholic ecumenical advances onward to new levels, since most of the people to whom he was asked to minister were non-Catholic. In undertaking this ministry he discovered what the essence of Catholicism and of Christianity really were. This was a singular and extremely important achievement, but it probably came about very naturally. One does not truly realize what is essential to Catholicism until one looks at it from another perspective, and the same is true of Protestantism. In discovering new perspectives, Henri Nouwen began to teach and exemplify a new type of Christianity that was for all Christians everywhere, and this happened at Yale.

2

THE PSYCHOLOGY
OF HENRI NOUWEN

The first chapter explored in some detail Henri Nouwen's origins in Holland and how it was that he came to public ministry in the United States. This early period could be considered his "hidden years." Although the first part of his life is not well known, it explains much of Henri's special perspective and situates him somewhat in the history of Christian life and spirituality. To lift the clouds yet further, I think the next aspect of Nouwen's life that must be addressed is his personality or psychology. This is important for a number of reasons, including the fact that Nouwen's spirituality is very much wrapped up in his own personal journey. When we read his works or remember his impassioned preaching, we are held fast by the human dimension of what he said. He preached what he was living and feeling.

Many people have wondered how they, too, might live this powerful message. There is even a new book, *Henri's Mantle*, by Chris Glaser,[1] which describes how one of Henri's friends is attempting to live Henri's way. I myself will admit that at one point I tried to simply imitate Henri, but I eventually learned that this did not work. Henri was able to "be" Henri Nouwen, but I doubt anyone else could actually do it. This realization led me to ask to what extent Henri Nouwen was a unique phenomenon. I wanted to know just *how* he is an example for others. I will return to this question later, but first it leads me to ask some serious questions about his psychology.

A further reason for delving into psychological issues is that Nouwen puzzled and exasperated many of the people who got to know him well or who worked with him closely. *Wounded Prophet*,[2] the most detailed biography of Henri to appear so far, is filled with negative observations regarding Henri's anxieties, problems, and contradictions—he was a "wounded" prophet; the title says it all. It must be admitted that, for all his high ideals and his wonderful message, Nouwen seems to have had some puzzling personal failings. Maybe he even had some mental or emotional condition that played into his difficulties. Whether or not this is true, I would, at the very least, like to know the reason for the deep uncertainty and feelings of worthlessness that he frequently told his friends about or alluded to in his writing. Where did these feelings come from? This important part of Henri can only be understood by taking a deeper look at his psychology.

A Special Person

I think that a proper beginning to any consideration of Henri Nouwen's psychology is to say that, despite his identification with humble people and many friendships with them, Henri Nouwen was far from being a "regular guy." Throughout most of his ministry he displayed a supercharged ability to do more and *be more* than "regular people" ever achieve. It was said, quite correctly, in the Nouwen biographical video, *Straight to the Heart*,[3] that he lived six lives in the space of one. What with his outsize charisma, drive, and sense of calling, he was closer psychologically to a politician or celebrated artist than to a typical priest or university professor. He belonged to that small group of people who are capable of standing out on the world stage and addressing or embodying our dreams and ideals. Henri was this sort of man, and the problems he suffered, as well as the disappointments and suffering he sometimes caused, are typical of the lives of those people who seem destined for notoriety or who accomplish much.

One of the clues that someone has this type of big personality is an early manifestation of purpose or of unusual abilities. In Henri's case, his later vocation was indeed indicated from early in his childhood. As we have seen, by the time he was six he had decided to become a priest, and at eight he had already begun to officiate in a toy chapel constructed in the family attic. The well-known American psychologist James Hillman has studied precociousness in persons of great talent or genius. According to Hillman, whether one looks to Judy Garland, Pablo Casals, Henry Ford, James Thurber, Harry Houdini, or any of the dozens of other figures he explores, there are early signs of their later famous abilities. Hillman believes that their characters are innate, and that they are expressing their "soul's code."[4]

Undeniably, certain people do manifest an unusual greatness of soul. They seem to meet just the right people or be in the right place at the right time. Call it destiny or a "lucky streak," there is a force that is displayed throughout their lives, sometimes even through events beyond their control. This is certainly not merely a matter of luck; such people, whether they are famous artists, composers, authors, or politicians often have a presence or an attractive charm, so much so that they seem to fill up a room when they enter it. They can be on stage facing thousands of people and feel comfortable and in charge. We must recognize that there *are* special people to whom special things happen. Although there are other much more famous examples, such as Winston Churchill or Elvis Presley, this same "mark of greatness" rested on Henri Nouwen. He had charisma.

I believe that Henri's charisma explains some of his greatness and his personal magnetism, but it also helps us to understand his faults, too. Like other similarly gifted people, Henri Nouwen was surprisingly uneven in his abilities. He could address some spiritual problem no one else could fathom, then become frustrated over some simple task like making a meal or packing a bag. A similar pattern can be seen in the lives of other charismatic figures. So much of their life's energy goes into the public persona that contradictions, weaknesses, and simple lack of understanding or development dog their more intimate affairs and relationships.

An example springs quickly to mind. Several years ago, a remarkably frank and surprising article entitled "Fame: The Power and Cost of a Fantasy" was published by Sue Erikson Bloland, the daughter of Eric Erikson.[5] It maintained that her father, an icon of developmental psychology and self-awareness, seemed on an intimate level to be quite devoid of the qualities he wrote about in his books. Within his family, he was a hollow man. Comparing her father to a few other great thinkers, artists, and politicians, Bloland finds that they, too, were flawed or incomplete at their core. If this is not unusual with other larger-than-life people, then, in Henri Nouwen's case, one might even expect to find at least as much impracticality, everyday incompetence, and uncertainty as he exhibited. These can be common characteristics of the celebrity and the artist.

The celebrity quality of Nouwen's life was paradoxical in that he preached against ambition and upward mobility and befriended very humble people. In fact, Nouwen made many deliberate moves to leave notoriety behind. He immersed himself in Cistercian monasteries, Latin American slums, and Ukrainian missions. The Daybreak community, where he ultimately found a home, was a very obscure destination. In his choice to work in these places, we see Nouwen's desire to avoid being swept up into the celebrity lifestyle, his tremendous adaptability, and his love for the common people of the world. We must also recognize that many of these obscure places became well known and were even changed because of Nouwen's presence there and his writing about them. *The Genesee Diary*, in which he wrote about his experience of solitude in a Cistercian monastery, was an epochal book for Henri Nouwen, one that increased his popularity and renown dramatically. Even when he sought obscurity, that same obscurity could be transformed into fame.

I believe that this celebrity quality is responsible in particular for the unevenness of his abilities. However, it only begins to answer all the questions people have asked about Henri Nouwen. I would like to explore several other notions or theories from the discipline of psychology that further illuminate both Nouwen's charisma and his emotional, highly engaged way of living.

Puer Aeternus

The second issue I want to explore now is one I have already mentioned briefly in regard to Henri Nouwen's difficulties in graduate school: his youthful spirit. Throughout his life, Nouwen displayed a childlike quality that managed to be both naïvely idealistic and yet wise at the same time. This "wise child" aspect of Henri was especially apparent when he was alone with friends. His l'Arche friend, Kathy Bruner, described it in this way:

> There was a great desire in his heart to know children and be creative, just to play in the sand or run in the waves where there would be no judgement. I saw a

great longing in him to be simple, to be loved for who
he was, to be carefree (which didn't come easily to
him). Yet at the same time he could be incredibly wise.[6]

Jungians have studied this personality type and constructed a
psychological profile of what they call the *puer aeternus*, a person who throughout life retains the qualities of a wise child.[7]
Like the Little Prince or Peter Pan, Henri was a *puer.* Like them,
he cast a spell on those around him, making it seem as if the
ordinary rules of life had been suspended. After all, those rules
were made by grown-ups, and Henri was not a grown-up.

Can we truly say that Nouwen was "*not* a grown-up"? Yes, I
believe we can. Remember, this was a man who celebrated his
sixtieth birthday by being reborn as a clown, a man who, at
roughly the same age, went off and joined the circus. He loved
parades and eating candy and all things that children love.
When he sat down to write his books, Henri always looked back
to his experiences as a boy or a teenager, for this was his field of
reference, his starting point. He once caught himself doing this.
While he was counseling a young man who had problems with
his parents, Henri was just starting to make an observation
about "the older generation" when he suddenly remembered
that he himself was old enough to be the boy's grandfather!
This was a not-uncommon experience for Henri Nouwen, who
typically saw himself as a youth. It came as great a surprise
when a core member of l'Arche looked at him on his birthday
and pronounced that he, Henri Nouwen, was an old man!

If we accept the possibility of a *puer* factor in Henri's character, then a large piece of the mystery of his psychology falls
away. We have already seen how *puer* issues figured in his difficulties in graduate school, and they ware indeed a factor
throughout his life and ministry. Henri conceived of maturity
and authority from a child's perspective, even very late in life.
For example, consider this passage written about a moment of

transcendence brought on by a near-death experience. He reflects back to a brief period of military service, which had thrust him into a position of hierarchy and regimentation:

> I felt I was taking off the wide leather belts that I had worn while chaplain with the rank of captain in the army. Those belts not only girded my waist but also crossed my chest and shoulders. They had given me prestige and power. They had encouraged me to judge people and put them in their place. Although my stay in the army was very brief, I had, in my mind, never fully removed my belts.[8]

Even as an older man, Henri thinks back on the feeling of being an army captain in *puer* terms. He remembers the belts he wore, and the psychological advantage they gave him, including the sense of power to judge and command others. Even his criticism of this juvenile fantasizing is itself a *puer* criticism: being judgmental is viewed here as dressing up in a uniform and taking on the commanding attitude of an army captain. For all the effectiveness of Henri's writing in this passage, this is *puer* thinking.

It was largely due to his *puer* nature that Henri was so charming and engaging. It was this same nature that helped him to see situations in a fresh light and to approach old issues with new vitality. The *puer* spirit is capricious, but it is serious, too. As Thomas Moore reminds us, "*puer* is not simply literal young age, but an attitude of youthfulness that may be full of spirit, ambition, high destiny, and a forgetfulness of mortality. It is a spirit that brings new life."[9] It is able to strip away the conventions and the half-truths that we all live by and take a fresh look, or make a new start.

That was Henri. He took every situation, every sermon, and every topic apart and reassembled it with some inspired or creative twist. He did not build on received wisdom, but dove down to the essence of whatever was before him. Although in this way Henri embodied the *puer* to a very remarkable degree, I think he also made a mighty effort to grow beyond a simple *puer* mentality. *Puers* do have limitations. His biggest break-through perhaps came when he wrote *The Return of the Prodigal Son*.[10] There, as he contemplated Rembrandt's image of the prodigal embraced by the aged father and the elder son looking on scornfully, he naturally began by identifying with the prodigal, who is the youngest figure in the tableau.

However, as his meditation progressed, he was able to see himself in the role of the elder brother, and finally he realized the need to "become the father," to take up the mantle of the one who provides shelter, grants forgiveness, and graces the lives of others. This acceptance of a fatherly capacity and mindset was a major growth step for Henri Nouwen and a de-parture from the *puer* perspective that was his mainstay. *The Return of the Prodigal Son* is so powerful, and is his finest book, in part because it represents enormous psychological growth regarding this very issue.

Personality Type

I want to move on now and look at Henri from another angle. The psychological model I find especially useful in arriving at a better understanding of Henri Nouwen is the Myers Briggs Typology Inventory, or MBTI. Many readers will be familiar with the Myers Briggs from its use in career development, workplace management, and church seminars and retreats. The MBTI is used broadly in the business world and among those interested in personal growth. Like the *puer* theory, it is also based on the research of Carl Jung and has been the most widely accepted element of his work.

According to this typology, everyone can be classified in terms of how they process information, their attitude toward the outside world, their manner of making decisions, and other such indicators. The MBTI is based on four pairs of opposing traits:

Attitude	Introversion	vs.	Extroversion
Function	I(N)tuition	vs.	Sensation
Function	Thinking	vs.	Feeling
Attitude	Judging	vs.	Perceiving

Everyone has some measure of all of these eight characteristics, but within each pair of opposites, most of us favor one over the other. Very briefly, let me explain some of these differences. Forgive me for making some quick generalizations in what I am about to say.

Introversion and Extroversion are concepts that have gained common currency. However, in psychological terms, what is most important about introverts is the extent to which their true frame of reference is inside themselves. They take a lot of information in and spend time mulling over and digesting it. Their response to these stimuli usually seems delayed, but it is worth the wait. Introverts can easily succumb to information overload. This and their slower response time can make them seem remote to others. Conversely, extroverts are people persons. They know what they think only when they hear themselves talking! It is by discussing and interacting that extroverts processes their lives. They keep very little secret, so what you see is what you get.

Intuition and Sensation have equally great differences. The intuitives are the bookish, more philosophical people among us. They like ideas and they wonder about future possibilities. Being so often caught up in such considerations, they are sometimes not fully aware of their immediate surroundings.

Sensing individuals are quite different. They excel at seeing and solving technical problems. They make great cooks, drivers, engineers, technicians, and builders. They are the people who make the world run, but the book you are now reading would probably not interest them at all.

The Thinking and Feeling categories refer to the way we make decisions. A thinker normally goes through a rational process to make a decision, while feelers rely on their inner sense of things and people. Feelers are much better than thinkers at relating to and understanding others, but thinkers can evaluate situations and usually explain themselves more clearly.

Finally, Judging and Perceiving are attitudes that relate most to how we process information. The Judging attitude is neater, likes things to be orderly, looks to closure, and even derives satisfaction from finishing a list of tasks. The Perceiving attitude, by contrast, is more easygoing and prefers to live and let live. Although those with a Perceiving attitude are more relaxed, they see things that the decisive Judging set might miss.

Notice that the top and bottom traits are *attitudes*, while those traits in the middle are *functions*. The traits are usually abbreviated to their first letter, with the exception of Intuition, which is known as "N." Depending on which of the eight characteristics we favor, we all end up fitting into one of sixteen four-letter combination groups, such as ISTP or ESTJ, etc.

If that were the extent of the MBTI, it would be of only limited interest, but it is at this point that the MBTI becomes truly remarkable. Each of the sixteen types yields a distinctly identifiable profile, a personality style that is much like the style of others of the same type. Each of these types, each of these groups of people, is on its own psychological journey through life, subject to inner pressures and priorities that are all its own.

So far I have said that Henri Nouwen was a *puer* and that he fit the profile of a celebrity type. I think that both these observations are helpful in understanding Henri. Can we go further and determine what his Myers Briggs type was, and whether he shares his type with any well-known figures? Let us try. With regard to Extroversion and Introversion, Henri had strong attributes in both directions, but he best fits the model of the extrovert; he got his energy from talking and sharing with others. As to Sensing or Intuition, Nouwen was a clear intuitive. Concerning Thinking or Feeling—which is not a test of intelligence, by the way—Nouwen was a feeler. He wrote volume after volume about how he felt and he easily empathized with others. Finally, Nouwen was not a regimented J, despite the influence of his organized Dutch upbringing, but a P, a perceiving type who lived outside the box.[11]

For the development of the rest of my argument concerning Myers Briggs typology I am going to rely heavily on a book called *Personality Type*, by Lenore Thomson.[12] When I read her section on the ENFP type, that is, on Extroverted Intuition with Feeling and Perception, it seemed like she must have known Henri Nouwen and was simply describing the man she remembered! I had not consulted this book with Henri in mind, but there he was, described and explained in detail. If Henri *was* a strong ENFP, then his charismatic personality and many of his mysterious and contradictory qualities may have been simply a part of his nature. ENFP individuals are frequently persons who attain greatness but do not escape their flaws. Bill Clinton is an ENFP, and I imagine that there are many other celebrity types who also fit this profile.

In order to really understand the psychological dynamic of Nouwen's life, we must go a bit deeper into MBTI theory, which I will try to summarize as best I can. According to the Myers Briggs theory, for each of the sixteen types there is a schema of four skill sets that are available to people of that type. These skill sets range from one's strongest to one's weakest ability. The strong set is developed earliest and is the dominant function used to deal with the world. Somewhat like being right- or left-handed, we develop our dexterity by having a leading or dominant skill set.

For an ENFP individual like Henri, the strongest skill set is Extroverted Intuition. There is also a weaker, introverted function, and that is Feeling, so Introverted Feeling is the secondary helping skill set of the ENFP. Below these in terms of availability and development is a third skill set, Extroverted Thinking. One's tertiary function is sometimes developed into consciousness only in the second half of life. There is a final fourth, inferior skill set that comes into play, but usually without any finesse or sophistication. For the ENFP, this is Introverted Sensation. Under pressure and unable to use any of one's more highly developed competencies, one turns to the inferior function, but the results are usually mixed. Our inferior function is our weak area.

Here, then, is Nouwen's ENFP skills schema, displayed in the typical, Myers Briggs "lasagna" fashion:

Dominant	Extroverted Intuition
Secondary	Introverted Feeling
Tertiary	Extroverted Thinking
Inferior	Introverted Sensation

Henri's Case

What does all this mean in practical terms? Well, if, like Henri Nouwen, one's primary skill set is Extroverted Intuition, then one takes in situations at a glance, not deeply, but globally, and one immediately senses what possibilities the future, or a few changes, might bring. The expression, "I have a gut feeling," comes closest to pegging this type of intuition. It is when someone—rightly or wrongly—gets a strong feeling about where something is headed. The word "intuitive" in this context does not mean that someone has a sixth sense or psychic powers. Lenore Thomson explains it perfectly:

> Whenever the word *intuitive* is applied to a genuine ENP, it's almost invariably followed by the word *promoter* or *communicator*. Such types strike us as "suited by nature" to sell themselves and their ideas. Charismatic, persuasive, and magnetic, ENPs are able to integrate diverse views in a larger pattern of meaning and to convince others that there are new and better ways of seeing reality. Steve Jobs, the visionary who turned a hacker's gadget into the Apple Computer industry, appears to be an excellent example of the type. So does Deepak Chopra, MD, author of many books on the integrated relationship of mind, body, and cosmos.[13]

This description fits Henri Nouwen, too, and helps explain his ability to rapidly scan huge issues, huge groups of people, and huge tasks and either get the gist of everything or focus in on the few things that interested him. Peter Weiskel, who was Nouwen's assistant at both Yale and Harvard, recalls with amusement the day Henri told him to "go get every book in print on Vincent van Gogh." Henri had no intention of reading all those books, but assembling them would help him see where to focus his attention. The ENFP has a style of engagement that resembles a camera, one that can take a wide-angle picture, then zoom in for a close-up.

Once these ENFP types zoom in, once they have their imaginations engaged by a project, a person, or an issue, they embrace it totally, sometimes in an almost romantic burst of passion, falling hopelessly and headlong into whatever it is. Issues and people can swallow them up, and yesterday's focus is forgotten. This is the psychological reason for Nouwen's famous ability to focus on a single person. That person received Nouwen's entire attention, and so did a series of subjects, from Thomas Merton to Latin America. Even if he was in a room crowded with people, the person to whom he was speaking felt Henri's attention was on him or her alone. The countless times when Nouwen got completely and surprisingly involved with another person's illness, or situation, or tragedy would have exhausted anyone else, but Henri's personality allowed him to do this easily. Indeed, it would have been difficult for him to have acted differently. This was one of his most endearing traits, and it left a lasting impression on others. Many people's lives were changed by the sense that Henri cared for them in some special way—and he *did* care. Consider this remembrance of Henri by television's Fred Rogers:

> He must have had huge phone bills because he called us—his friends—from all over the world. He'd usually start out by saying, "Hello, Fred. This is Henri." In fact, he'd talk so quickly it most often sounded like, "Hello, Fred…Henri." I'd ask him where he was, and he'd say Toronto or Holland or Russia or California or England or Santa Fe, but then he'd get right to his point: *"How are you?"* He always wanted to know how I was. When my best friend from high school was dying, Henri would invariably ask, "And how is Jim doing?" He even called Jim and his wife and asked *them*, "How are you?" And he really wanted to know. He wanted to be connected with all of us in the most essential ways.[14]

Also, because of this focusing ability, an ENFP like Henri Nouwen usually impresses others as a visionary idealist. Such a person appears absolutely confident, completely certain of what he or she is saying, and able to convince others of why they should accept his or her brilliant new vision! This is the perfect person to become an evangelist, or even an inventor. The downside is that such passionate interest burns bright and then usually burns out. This kind of focused, romantic certainty can last only so long. Once the audience gets the message, or the product hits the shelf, an ENFP usually moves on, loses interest, and can even go into a slump. This is a very important point to consider with regard to Henri Nouwen. His occasional depressions were painful, and this helps to explain them. Nouwen was so often up or down that in the early stages of preparing this chapter I had to consider the possibility that there was a manic depressive element to Henri's psychology. However, I have decided that his roller coaster emotional dips can probably be attributed most simply to his reliance on Intuition to make his way in the world.

Another difficulty that arises out of reliance on Intuition is a lack of patience and follow-through. This was certainly an issue with Henri, one I have discussed in a previous publication. There I wrote: "Henri left the details and the follow-up to others, to the grown-ups; what he offered us was a unique opportunity to really live the spirit of the gospel, to reach out, to really let go."[15] Well, "leaving the details and follow-up to others," as I wrote then, must have been firmly in his charts, because I found an almost identical characterization in Thomson's description of the ENFP personality:

> Such types are so flexible and so quick to grasp the essence of the situation that they can do just about anything they set their minds to. But they may not stick with a situation long enough to realize the fruits of their labors. They depend on their supporters to take care of the follow-through and detail work, and those supporters wind up reaping the harvest.[16]

So Intuition, in Nouwen's case, not only fed his uniquely artistic and spiritual view of the world, it also was a big part of his famous restlessness. It even helps explain the peculiar un-evenness in Henri's life. ENFPs are so quick to form an intuitive impression of things that they do not develop real knowledge or judgment. This results in periodic experiences of anxiety when life seems to have no meaning. It also leads to over-extension and an exasperating inability to deal with close relationships. ENFPs assume that other people are able to anticipate their needs and they often expect too much from others and from themselves. Again, Thomson notes:

> ENPs don't recognize that they are overextending themselves. Without sufficient Judgment, they believe their intentions are as good as realized. It's just a matter of adding water, connecting the dots, filling in the blanks. They may not even start a project until the deadline has already passed. In consequence, ENPs are both surprised and frustrated by the problems that arise when their best intentions collide with material reality. They feel a sense of injustice, as though life were being unfair to them. Indeed, these types can be badly hurt when people call them on promises they're not able to keep. After all, their heart was in the right place. It's circumstances that have changed. Extreme ENP's may even deny behaviors that have met with others' disap-proval. An admission of wrongdoing would suggest that they *intended* to do wrong, and they didn't. The behaviors felt right to them at the time.

> People who rely too heavily on their Intuition are usually caught between the devil and the deep blue sea. Unwilling to acknowledge their own limitations, they're forced to depend on the limits of others. Even-tually life confronts them with problems Intuition can't

handle, and their psyche pressures them to grow. They feel the unexpected pull of their inferior function, Introverted Sensation.[17]

As I said previously, the inferior function is our weak area, that part we never get right. Despite some saintly attitudes and accomplishments, Henri certainly had his weak areas. In particular, there was an envious or resentful spirit that he could not shake. When one reads through any of the more revealing passages in a Nouwen book, it can be surprising to see Henri admit to problems of resentment or envy or lack of fulfillment. This undercurrent in his personality seems odd, considering that he was so successful both in the world and at reforming his own heart, but these problems were there. For example, near the end of his life he wrote something that really surprised me:

I know that my sorrows are mine and will not leave me. In fact I know they are very old and very deep sorrows, and that no amount of positive thinking or optimism will make them less. The adolescent struggle to find someone to love me is still there; unfulfilled needs for affirmation as a young adult remain alive in me. The deaths of my mother and many family members and friends during my later years cause me continual grief. Beyond all that, I experienced deep sorrow that I have not become who I wanted to be, and that the God to whom I have prayed so much has not given me what I have most desired.[18]

Although he begins in a realistic, confessional tone, a bit of resentment and self-pity begins to surface as this passage progresses: How was he able to say, after living such a wonderful life, that he never became who he wanted to be, or that his greatest desire was never fulfilled? Then he lets off a little of his anger by blaming God, "to whom I have prayed so much," for the latter problem. Through this momentary slip we see an expression of the resentful, unforgiving, small side of Henri. We see the tendency to project the problem onto others, in this case, God, and to not take responsibility. All this smacks of the inferior function.

Inferior Introverted Sensation is self-centered but self-doubtful, and even slightly paranoid. It is a modality that remains primitive and childish. When this function gets triggered, projections outward usually follow. The problem then seems to ENFPs to not lie with themselves, but to be out there—it is the friends who do not call, it is the colleagues who are unsupportive, it is the editors who are trying to control the process or are too demanding. Henri, like other ENFPs, needed a high level of approval and support from others, and he could easily become resentful and bitter if this was not forthcoming. These problems emanated from Introverted Sensation.

Thomson explains:

> ENPs don't see their Introverted Sensate impulses as part of themselves. Under pressure from this part of themselves, they suspect that others aren't supporting them well enough, and they lose faith in their ability to change things, to explore new possibilities. People who question their motives or behaviors strike them as spoilers, attempting to rein them in, control them, or deprive them of approval.
>
> ENPs in this situation generally respond to the perceived problem by pushing the envelope. They test people's limits, attempting to force an expression of unconditional love and approval. What they actually need is more experience with their secondary function, Introverted Thinking or Introverted Feeling. When ENPs feel personally responsible [for] the situation

they create, they set limits for themselves, and they're not so dependent on others' approval and reactions.[19]

These last words are very important. In Thomson's remarks we find expressed the goal of Henri's psychological journey, and the journey of any ENFP: Instead of focusing on the betrayals and the unwillingness of others to understand or to support them, under pressure ENFPs must rely on their secondary skill set, on Introverted Feeling. That is, they must rediscover the inner values that truly guide their lives. Henri Nouwen suffered chronically over hurt feelings and disappointment: that his father never read his books, that certain friends did not accept his advice or his invitations to travel with him, or that his best friend Nathan needed some space from Henri's needs for intimacy. The list goes on and on.

The quarrel he had with Nathan Ball at l'Arche Daybreak caused Nouwen to go into complete psychological freefall. He collapsed and needed to undergo a long and intense psychological evaluation and treatment. He emerged from that ordeal by turning within, to his own deeper self, and to what he held to be true. This is exactly what Thomson would have recommended. He needed to stop focusing on what other people might say, either for or against him, and listen to his own heart. He eventually published the secret journal of his recovery, aptly titled *The Inner Voice of Love*. Here is a passage from that book in which he exhorts himself to continue the inward focus that was so essential:

> When you discover in yourself something that is a gift from God, you have to claim it and not let it be taken away from you. Sometimes people who do not know your heart will altogether miss the importance of something that is part of your deepest self, precious in your eyes as well as God's. They might not know you

well enough to be able to respond to your genuine needs. It is then that you have to speak your heart and follow your own deepest calling.

There is a part of you that too easily gives in to others' influence. As soon as someone questions your motives, you start doubting yourself. You end up agreeing with the other before you consult your own heart. Thus you go passive and simply assume that the other knows better.

Here you have to be very attentive to your inner self.[20]

From a psychological perspective, this advice Henri gives to himself is absolutely sound, yet it required of him a difficult detaching from a myriad of external forces, particularly people in authority, his closest friends, and important associates. He needed to turn inward to consult his own values. Henri found his deepest personal truth in his love of Jesus, and in his deep certainty that he, like Jesus, was also God's beloved. As long as he remained faithful to that core, he was able to be the prophet of the love of God that he was called to be.

I have relied heavily on the MBTI in writing this chapter because it sheds so much light on Henri's surprising combination of greatness and weakness, vision and vulnerability. I believe that a good number of the more puzzling aspects of his personality can be explained as aspects of the ENFP personality type. By this I am saying that Nouwen was probably much more psychologically healthy than even he himself suspected. Many of the concerns that most bothered him can be understood as authentic parts of his personality, rather than elements of a neurosis or a psychological condition. ENFPs make up roughly 10 percent of the population, so Henri was like many other people—only more so!

Let us pause for a moment to put this information in spiritual perspective. As I said at the beginning of this chapter, it is not advisable for anyone today to follow Henri Nouwen by simply acting like Henri. It should be clear at this point why that approach does not work. Much of Henri's charm, his penetrating insight, his passion, and his sorrow were natural expressions of his ENFP personality. The fact that he was such a strong ENFP was also the source of some of Henri's more Christ-like attitudes, such as his willingness to pull up stakes and move on to some new place for the sake of the gospel, his ardent concern for individuals in need, his fresh and sometimes amazingly insightful perspective, and his ability to move easily outside the box and beyond the rules.

Considering Henri from the vantage point of the MBTI also reveals the locus of his greatest temptation and the direction his spiritual and psychological growth needed to take. Nouwen had to develop his secondary (Introverted Feeling) and tertiary (Extroverted Thinking) skill sets. It was through Introverted Feeling that he was able to connect to his own inner values and his God. Once there, he was unshakeable and truly inspired. Nouwen made his journey, and his example encourages all of us to make our own journeys. This is the way we are best able to follow in his footsteps: by moving down our own paths.

Shame

While I have concluded that most of Henri's issues were expressions of character, I must now add an important caveat: Henri often experienced levels of anxiety that were not entirely normal. To do justice to the subject of Henri's psychology, we must also briefly consider his anxiety problem. Why was he occasionally seized with doubt or despair, or paralyzed with fear that nothing he did mattered, that he would be abandoned, or even that no one would be present at his funeral?

These strong feelings that often plagued him sprang from shame. Psychologically, shame is somewhat like guilt. However, if guilt means feeling bad about what you have done, then shame means feeling bad about who you are. According to many psychologists, wherever strong feelings of shame are present, then there was someone, usually a parent, who instilled those feelings of shame; there was a "shamer."

Henri and some of the people around him have wondered if this shaming figure in Henri's life was his father, who may have unwittingly instilled such feelings in Henri by being too hard on him or by ignoring his sensitivities or need for affirmation. His father's admiration for and pursuit of excellence never sat well with Henri. Being the son of this lawyerly, professorial father was a fundamental factor in Nouwen's life, shaping him in many positive ways, but also creating in him deep feelings of frustration and resentment. In 1984, when Henri's anger at his father was finding more open expression, he took a deep dig at him with the words, "You had very little sympathy for people whom you considered 'failures.' The weak did not attract you."[21] In Henri's mind, he himself was one of those failures; he thought he never measured up in his father's eyes.

These feelings were never constant, and Nouwen was more and more reconciled to his father later in life. However, there were many years of torment for Henri over his inability to please his father or to communicate with him on a deep level. I myself remember that even late in his life Henri would complain to me and to other friends about his father, whom he felt did not support him or understand him and who was always overly concerned with accomplishments and achievements.

Once Henri tried to explain his father to me. He chose as an example his father's inability to comprehend why he would even think about joining l'Arche: "You see, for my father, a person you can really respect and admire is someone of great wit and intellect, who can craft the perfect argument." Henri said this without anger—this was just the way his father was. Laurent Nouwen did delight in a fine argument and in anyone who was a master of language and debate. This ideal was, of course, the complete opposite of the people at l'Arche, and it does not closely describe Henri Nouwen, either, despite his verbal skills.

Some of the people who listened to Henri's complaints assumed that Henri's father's insensitivity was extreme enough to qualify as clinical narcissism. It is true that Henri exhibited some of the classic traits of the child of a narcissist, known from Alice Miller's many books and captured with special clarity in Elan Golomb's *Trapped in the Mirror: Adult Children of Narcissists in Their Struggle for Self.*[22] Children of narcissists have special problems in claiming their own identity and in knowing their own worth. Was this the key to Henri's sense of shame? Certainly there are reasons to consider this possibility.

But perhaps there is another reason for these feelings. In searching for an answer to this question, I have had help from someone who was very involved in the family dynamic and has also thought deeply about the matter, Henri's youngest brother, named Laurent like his father.

With both his parents and Henri now gone, Laurent Jr. has watched the growing consensus of opinion regarding Henri and his parents with a certain uneasiness. In a letter to me he wrote, "that relationship gets stereotyped more and more. Relativity disappears, as if it was a black-and-white situation lasting a solid 64 years. Unfortunately, in this process my father is more and more described as an insensitive, rational, ambitious, intellectual hardliner and my mother as a saint devoted to religion."[23] Laurent Jr. admits that this stereotyping has even played a part in the family's own reflections. His brother Paul and his sister Laurien have both spoken in similar terms about Henri and his father. Indeed, the stereotype, if there is one, goes back to Henri's own statements and reflections.

However, Laurent Jr.'s more thoughtful, more neutral views have led me beyond an overly simplified and even polarized sketch of Henri's family. From everything I have gathered, I believe that Laurent Sr. can be understood as a man of determination, high standards, and energy who was probably more concerned with his own life and his own agenda than with those of anyone else. He was probably not so much a narcissist as self-absorbed. Many fathers fit this description.

When we consider Henri's views of his father, on the other hand, we must keep in mind that Henri's siblings turned out very differently from the way he did, and that Henri's shame and the ENFP tendency toward distrustful projections and "paranoia" colored and distorted his view of reality. Frankly, I doubt that he could see his father clearly. Much of his anger and disappointment over his father may have been due to Henri's own deep sensitivity and his high expectations for friends and family.

Shame is a mysterious human condition, rooted more than anything else in the sensitivity of the person to events happening around him or herself. Henri had some early predisposition to shame. To make matters more difficult, he grew up in a religious culture that actively promoted feelings of shame and guilt. The examination of conscience and the weekly confession of sins required by the Catholic Church throughout Henri's youth and young adulthood did nothing to alleviate his sense that he was no good, damaged, or unworthy of acceptance and love.

In addition to being sensitive and prone to self-doubt, Henri slowly came to an uneasy awareness that he was homosexual, and this can hardly have added to his sense of well-being. Although there have been great changes in the societal view of homosexuality in the last ten years, particularly in Holland, Henri saw few of these changes in his own lifetime. Homosexuality was officially listed as a disorder or a disease in the United States until 1973.[24] It is still considered to be such by the Catholic Church.[25] In the thirties, forties, and fifties, homosexuality was a feared, even loathsome aberration—part sin, part mental illness. No one talked about it except as a joke or an insult. Even in Henri's family, his sexual orientation was not discussed until late in his life. In his youth it constituted a problematic and painful secret that kept Henri from experiencing many types of intimacy with others. He knew he was not like other people and that he did not dare reveal this truth about himself.

While homosexual guilt probably contributed to Nouwen's sense of shame as he became older and perhaps exacerbated tensions with his father, questions of sexual identity come to a head during puberty. Henri's sense of shame was rooted in something more basic. There was an innate disposition and an early layer of traumatic experience in Henri's life, one occurring at such an early time that, psychologically speaking, neither sexual identity nor the father figure were really dominant factors. As his friend, the psychologist Peter Naus, wrote:

> As I see it, the primary issue in Henri's case was...a deep-seated insecurity, a sense that he was not securely connected to the people around him, including the significant others in his life. I have often wondered about the source of this insecurity but have never found a convincing answer. The only thing I am certain of is that it lay in the distant past.[26]

Elsewhere, Naus went further:

> Henri had not been securely attached, in the sense that he always seemed to be searching for affection

and was never quite sure if people appreciated him. Yet the mother-son relationship suggests a very strong attachment—so why was it broken? One possibility is that, for whatever reason, Henri almost at birth had a need for security, affection and love that exceeded by far what could normally be provided for a child. There was something early in his life, outside the control of mother or father, which somehow threatened that bond.[27]

Peter Naus is suggesting that there was an almost primordial imbalance in Henri's relationship to the world. I agree. From the beginning, Henri would have had the ENFP's special concerns for support and approval, and this was coupled with an uncomfortable sense of shame and abandonment. Because Henri indeed felt shame at a fundamental level of his psyche, he looked to his friends and family and especially to his parents for reassurance. He alludes to this in *Here and Now*.

When I was a small child I kept asking my father and mother: "Do you love me?" I asked that question so often and so persistently that it became a source of irritation to my parents. Even though they assured me hundreds of times that they loved me I never seemed fully satisfied with their answers and kept on asking the same question.[28]

Later in the passage Henri goes on to relate this doubt to a fear of death and to his hope that his parent's love might save him from it, but this appears to be a later amplification. His basic feeling was one of shame and unworthiness, an issue that, according to many theorists, makes its appearance in young children between eighteen months and three years of age.[29] This was indeed an early and a basic problem.

Therefore, I think it is most likely that a good deal of Henri's frustration with his father was not due primarily to any supposed narcissism on the part of his father, but rather to Henri's own early and deep-seated sense of shame and need for reassurance. Henri was a highly sensitive, ENFP child, and there was simply not enough unqualified support in his environment to quiet his apprehensions. His siblings emerged without the same issues. Henri was forever asking too much of his relationships with others, and his relationship with his father was no exception. He needed something, some assurance, some level of profound acceptance, that Laurent Sr. could not always give him. As Laurent Jr. writes,

> I sometimes believe that my father accepted Henri much more than Henri could recognize. There was a reaching out to Henri that the good old man did in his own way, with his own set of references and hang-ups, etc. But Henri had difficulty with his unsatisfied desire to reach the depths of someone else's person, in this case, the depths of my father. I have to admit that sometimes I had the same kind of problems with Henri during his many visits to our home. It was hard for him to accept that I had to live my own life the way I thought best and that I was not able to live it as intensely every moment as he thought I should be living.[30]

I have dwelt on Nouwen's anxiety at length because it is fundamental to any spiritual evaluation of Henri Nouwen. All those who knew Henri well can tell stories of irrational waves of insecurity and fear of rejection that occasionally erupted in the midst of their otherwise pleasant times with him, and how surprised they were to sense such insecurity in someone who gave and received so much from the world. The quintessential wounded healer, Nouwen offered a great gift to the world in spite of his own difficult emotional life. In this he was like his fellow Dutchman, Vincent van Gogh. We must remember that much good came from Henri's troubles. Indeed, his sensitivity and his woundedness were his entrée into a perspective of humility and solidarity with all those who are poor in spirit.

Henri's difficulties remind us that God can use anyone and, in fact, God often chooses persons whose weaknesses are more obvious to bear the gospel. St. Paul mentions this issue frequently. In his letters, Paul alludes at several points to God choosing what is weak to shame the strong, to being weak in Christ, and says that when he is weak, then he is strong.[31] Henri learned, as Paul did, to accept his troubles and weaknesses and see in them God's presence and purpose. Henri developed an ability to work with his limitations and integrate or "befriend" them.

Laying Open His Life

I wonder what Henri would make of this chapter about his weaknesses. Perhaps the topic would have made him uneasy. What I have tried to do is investigate and explain what seem to me, and to perhaps many others, some puzzling aspects of his life. Henri didn't like to be categorized, and may not have agreed with all that I have said, but he would have welcomed the attempt to understand him and pay some attention to the more sensitive areas of his life. He not only wrote about them himself, he thought that by revealing his life he was following Jesus and was even "laying down his life" for others to see and learn:

> As good shepherds we are called to lay down our lives for our people. This laying down might in special circumstances mean dying for others. But it means first of all

making our own lives—our sorrows and joys, our despair and hope, our loneliness and experience of intimacy—available to others as sources of new life. One of the greatest gifts we can give others is ourselves.[32]

I believe that understanding Henri's special gifts is a big part of living within his legacy to us. Henri teaches us that we grow in holiness by becoming more completely ourselves and acknowledging our authentic feelings and failures. Although Henri was a complex figure, his message of God's love for us remained simple. That a complex man like Henri could bear such a simple message so well and touch so many is itself a teaching about God's ways and the ministry of the weak among us.

3
AN ARTIST, NOT A SCRIBE

A Spirit of Creativity

We have now considered Henri Nouwen's psychology in some depth and found a few concepts that may illuminate some of the interesting and perhaps even the more puzzling aspects of his personality. To take our inquiries further, I propose that we now turn to Henri's method of doing theology. Of course, just as he was not aware of the influence of his Dutch origins or of any of the pieces of his psychological puzzle I have tried to identify, Henri was not conscious that he was using any particular theological method. Nevertheless, I believe that there was a style or an approach that Henri Nouwen usually employed, and we can learn a great deal by understanding what it was.

When I think of Henri's message and his spirit, what strikes me most is his vivid authenticity and originality. Although he worked with traditional subjects and kept to a plain and simple level of communication, Henri nevertheless created a new spirituality. Considered a traditionalist by many, he actually transformed every topic he touched. Whatever the subject was, he took it to a new and higher level. His simple books and letters shine with originality and freedom.

I believe that this is one of the most important things we can say about his method. For an ecclesiastical writer, Henri Nouwen displays an unusual level of creativity, even what we might call "artistic license." Although Henri was not an artist, I use the word "artistic" deliberately. I do so because there is a strong artistic element in Henri Nouwen's approach to theology and to life.

For one thing, Henri Nouwen identified strongly with art and with artists. He spent hours, days, and weeks studying and reflecting on paintings and other artwork, and he commissioned several works of art himself. He was particularly fascinated by the icons of Eastern Christianity, and that is also very interesting. Icons, different from the great religious paintings of the West, are thought to embody and impart the spirit of the person or scene portrayed. They are holy objects, windows into a deeper reality, and some icons are even considered miraculous.

Let me explain a little further. Despite the biblical prohibition against worship before graven images, the creation of icons became common in the first centuries of early Christianity. The Eastern Church eventually justified the use of icons on the grounds that the Incarnation had transformed all of creation, and all of materiality, making ordinary physical objects into worthy vessels for the sacred spirit of what the holy icons portrayed. Nouwen not only used icons in his prayer life and wrote about them in his *Behold the Beauty of the Lord*,[1] he also grasped the central paradox of the iconographer's work—the fact that icons are not painted, but are "written"; that is what the Greek root, "graph," means. The icons are taken down, or "written," as faithful copies of earlier icons, going back to the original, yet each icon is invariably a new artistic work, created in a prayerful and attentive attitude of mind and heart. Icons are faithful transmissions, artistically rendered. This was how Henri approached his subjects as well, with a respect for tradition and an openness to transformation.

In fact, if one thinks of his books as icons instead of spiritual conferences, they even appear to function in the same way that icons do, or as any great work of art in the West does. As happens with art, Nouwen's books inspire, transform, and open up new perspectives for his readers. Like an artist or an iconographer, he speaks directly to people's hearts. Also, like many artists, he engages with his work both emotionally and personally, often to the point that the line between writer and subject blur and one merges with the other. In the end, objectivity can disappear in Nouwen's work, but what takes its place is a vision of a renewed and transformed Christianity, a vision born of both deep contemplation and a remarkable freedom to reinterpret and remake what Henri saw before him.

Henri Nouwen clearly had an inspired, artistic side to him, and I am convinced that his treatment of Christian themes is compelling and original precisely because it springs from a fundamentally artistic temperament or consciousness. How did Henri come to this artistic awareness? It certainly was not a part of his seminary or university training. Perhaps if we can find out who or what influence on Henri led him in this direction, that might help us see how his vision was born and developed. But before dealing with influences on Henri Nouwen, let me explain further what I mean by an "artistic approach."

A Classic Example

When reading spiritual and religious writers, I find that their method, or what they hope to accomplish, usually is to explain and expound topics without introducing changes or distortions. Originality is not usually their goal, nor is too much original thinking valued very highly. For one thing, most religious writers are constrained by a desire to remain orthodox in regard to doctrinal matters. Concerning the interpretation of scripture, such writers want to engage in descriptive "exegesis," which means bringing things out of the text, rather than "eisegesis," which means putting things into it. Their usual approach is rational, descriptive, and sober. It can sometimes even be rather cautious.

The usual approach to religious writing is fundamentally different from the artistic approach. Dancers, musicians, poets, and visual artists—at least the important ones—all seem to begin from another starting point, one with different priorities that allows for much greater freedom, even if they are producing sacred art. I will give you an example: One of the most beautiful and probably most renowned images of Jesus and Mary is Michelangelo's statue, the *Pietà*. It depicts Jesus in death, lying across Mary's lap. Many believe this is the most sublime piece of Christian art ever created. The *Pietà* certainly has few equals and it can reveal many deep truths as one meditates on it.

However, when contemplating the *Pietà*, one cannot proceed in a literal fashion. Although Michelangelo's statue is rightly acclaimed as a pinnacle of Christian artistry, the *Pietà* must nevertheless be deemed a failure if judged according to the canons of historical or technical accuracy. You may find this surprising, but consider the following observation: the scene that Michelangelo portrays is not found in any gospel, canonical or noncanonical. The records of early Christianity make no mention of Mary ever holding the dead body of Jesus.

However, if we accept that this powerful scene is not exactly historical, it becomes easier to see that in the *Pietà* Michelangelo may actually be invoking a number of different moments in the gospel story all at once. One of these moments obviously is the death of Jesus. When Jesus died, his mother was present. The story of Mary beneath the cross is found in the Gospel of

John. The *Pietà* is a worthy monument to Mary's faithfulness to Jesus even at his death. Nevertheless, the *Pietà* is not merely a meditation on the last moments of Jesus. We can see this by looking more closely at Mary. Her face in the *Pietà* is not the face of an older woman; it is the face of a young girl. Michelangelo has made Mary look even younger than Jesus in this scene. The size of her figure is also out of proportion to his. If Jesus is a man of normal stature, then the Mary of the *Pietà* must be eight or nine feet tall. What Michelangelo is really doing by giving Mary a young girl's face and such a large body is blending into the death of Jesus another image, that of the Madonna and Child, one of the great icons of Christian faith.

Michelangelo is superimposing the image of the Madonna onto the image of the Cross. Then, he gracefully brings in yet another moment in the gospel. If we reflect on Mary's expression and the way she is extending her hand, we are put most in mind of the Annunciation, and the words "Let it be so unto me." The face of Mary is the face of the Annunciation, not one of grief, but one of graceful acquiescence. So what Michelangelo has done in the *Pietà* is to transmit the whole story of Jesus and Mary in a single image—the Annunciation, the Madonna and Child, and the Crucifixion are all portrayed together. They are all part of the *Pietà*, blending into a single rich tapestry of stone, containing layer upon layer of insight into Mary's central role in the Incarnation.

This is artistic expression. It is neither factual nor intellectual. The viewer is drawn in and learns something about Mary and Jesus by a process that is contemplative and spiritual rather than mental. To create this image, what Michelangelo did was evoke a whole series of scenes in the gospel by making changes and combinations, by fusing together scenes and motifs that were originally separate. In the end, Michelangelo was both boldly original and faithful to the spirit of the Bible, if not to the letter.[2]

Henri Nouwen's way through a topic has many of these same qualities. This is seen most clearly when Henri deals with a biblical theme, just as in the case of Michelangelo. Henri's way through the Bible is selective and synthetic; that is, he brings ideas and themes together from many different places. Some of the connections he finds are quite remarkable. They are almost hidden in the text, so that it is only Henri's deep engagement with the things of God that seems to have led him to discover them in the first place.

Explorations in John's Gospel

Let us look at an example of how Henri brings themes out of the text of the Bible, in this case, the Gospel of John. Henri became engaged with John's gospel, especially later in life, because he found in that mystical gospel a resonance with his own passionate spirituality. In this instance, a remark by Jean Vanier, the founder of l'Arche, led Henri to develop an extended meditation on a trio of words, "intimacy, fecundity, ecstasy,"[3] a meditation that he explored in his book, *Lifesigns*, and elsewhere.

> Speaking of himself as the vine and of his disciples as the branches, Jesus says: "Make your home in me, as I make mine in you" (John 15:4). This is an invitation to intimacy. Then he adds: "Those who remain in me with me in them, bear fruit in plenty" (John 15:5). This is a call to fecundity. Finally, when he says, "I have told you this so that my own joy may be complete" (John 15:11), he promises ecstasy. The more I read and reflected on the Gospel of John, the more I became aware of the importance of these themes. Once alerted to them by Jean Vanier, I recognized them as golden threads woven through the whole of John's gospel.[4]

Even in such a brief passage we see Henri's expansive meditative process at work: he quotes the gospel as saying, "Make
your home in me," although the biblical text of 15:4 actually
reads, "Remain in me." He is expanding the sense of the text,
and the idea of a home, a place to live, is one he has taken from
an earlier verse. In the previous chapter Jesus had used a word
for "home" twice, though that word is usually translated as
"dwelling place": "Whoever loves me will keep my word, and
my Father will love him, and we will come to him and make
our *home* with him."[5] Earlier in the gospel there had been another passage following this theme that reads, "In my Father's
house there are many *places to live*,"[6] many "homes."

Henri, in his creative meditation on John's gospel, draws
the two images together, the one that promises a room or a
home in the house of God and the other that refers to being a
branch on the vine of Jesus, and he fuses them into a call to
settle in and dwell with God. Then Henri goes further, claiming that "making a home in Jesus" is a theme running through
the gospel. He is right in what he says, although commentators
have never really noticed this theme before. The idea is there,
however. Consider, for example, that in one of the opening
scenes of John's gospel we find not only the important statement that Jesus "dwelt" among us,[7] but also an invitation to
stay in the home of Jesus.

In that scene two disciples of John the Baptist start to follow
Jesus as he begins to walk away. He asks them, "What are you
looking for?" They in turn ask him, "Rabbi, where are you staying?" (This is the same word in Greek that Henri translates as
"make your home.") Jesus says to them, "Come and you will
see." Then, the gospel tells us, "they went with him and saw
where he was *staying* and *stayed* with him that day."[8] Henri isn't
simply forcing two images together by having the gospel say,
"Make your home in me." He is actually drawing the whole

gospel together around the "golden thread" of "remaining, stay-ing" or "making a home" with Jesus. In Greek it is all the same word, and the idea comes up at regular intervals in the gospel.

Henri does not leave the matter there. He goes further. He wants to make John's gospel a call not merely to dwell with Jesus, but to experience intimacy and even ecstasy with him. Again, Henri's instincts appear to be correct, even if no one has ever seen this point as clearly as he does. Is this not the gospel in which the author, "John," reclines with his head on the chest of Jesus, and is "John" not said to be especially beloved by Jesus? Any biblical scholar would agree that this bond, this claim of intimacy between Jesus and "John," is right at the heart of the mystical fourth gospel.

When Jesus looks down from the cross at this beloved dis-ciple in John's gospel, he says that Mary will be his mother and calls John her son. Mary goes to live *in his house*. Jesus, Mary, and the beloved disciple do share intimacy and become like a family. "Ecstasy" sounds like mystical rapture available only to a sainted few, but Henri makes it clear that he is interested in the fourth gospel's promise of joy. Complete joy is what Jesus brings to us, and this joy is a real kind of ecstasy:

> "Ecstasy" comes from the Greek "ekstasis," which in turn is derived from "ek," meaning out, and "stasis," a state of standstill. To be ecstatic literally means to be outside of a static place. Thus, those who live ecstatic lives are always moving away from rigidly fixed situa-tions and exploring new, unmapped dimensions of re-ality. Here we see the essence of joy. Joy is always new. Whereas there can be old pain, old grief, and old sor-row, there can be no old joy. Old joy is not joy! Joy is always connected with movement, renewal, rebirth, change—in short, with life.[9]

So Henri has brought out themes only latent in the gospel and given them new clarity and power by fusing them together. He has done this through a meditation that expands artistically on the text. This is very much like what Michelangelo does in the *Pietà*. In both cases the vision springs from the depths of the gospel itself, but synthesizes into something new.

When Henri moves into the biblical text, he sees it globally, and, like many artists, he finds his own wounded yet hopeful self within its story. Let us follow him as he carries his meditation on dwelling with Jesus further in another book, and notice how his own personal self-awareness becomes part of the tapestry he is weaving.

> In the house of my father there are many places to live...Each child of God has there his or her unique place, all of them places of God. I have to let go of all comparison, all rivalry and competition, and surrender to the Father's love. This requires a leap of faith because I have little experience of non-comparing love and do not know the healing power of such a love. As long as I stay outside in the darkness, I can only remain in the resentful complaint that results from my comparisons ...God is urging me to come home, to enter into his light, and to discover there that, in God, all people are uniquely and completely loved. In the light of God I can finally see my neighbor as my brother, as the one who belongs to God as much as I do.[10]

Light, darkness, the immeasurable love of the Father for the world, returning home to God, and becoming a child of God in a place uniquely prepared for me—these are all themes found somewhere in John, but Henri brings them together in a new and compelling way. What Henri is doing with this gospel is bringing to the surface underlying motifs that are contained within the story but are not necessarily clear or obviously connected. This is how artists always handle ideas and images. They expand themes, they weave in reflections and join disconnected bits and pieces into a new vision of the whole.

Sitting at God's Table

Let me give another example of Nouwen's method, this time not concerning scripture so much as doctrine. Before Henri left on what would be his final journey to Russia, a journey that was interrupted by his death, he prepared for mailing to many of his friends a signed copy of one of the books he had written while on sabbatical, *Can You Drink the Cup?* It was a poignant moment for me, and I imagine for many others, to open my mailbox after he was gone and find the familiar-looking package with the Henri Nouwen return address among my other mail. Receiving another book from Henri made it seem like his dying had not ended his ministry at all. Although I had not read all the books Henri had sent me over the years, I immediately sat down and read this one, which deals with the simple but celebratory act of drinking. Henri tells us that to "drink the cup," especially as Eucharist, is always a celebration. It is a doorway leading to real appreciation for life in our flesh, in our families, on our piece of ground and our time, and it is also a reckoning with death.

While in the process of writing this book, Henri had shared with me that he would be dealing with several Old Testament passages. We talked especially about the night of the "writing on the wall," when the use of the sacred cup by foreign conquerors had led to the death and destruction of these transgressors.[11] So, when I read the book, I laughed to see how in Henri's skilled hands the Old Testament readings had been transformed into a uniquely personal reflection on the life Henri had led, the many cups he had held in his hands, and what it had meant to raise these cups in the name of Jesus and in the name of life. In the finished book nothing remained of our conversation that was technical, abstract, "out there," or far from our own flesh and experience. Henri had taken one of the most overgrown and impossible of topics, the Eucharist, and said something true and pure and new. Like Jesus, Henri had this great talent for honing down big topics and speaking the simple, intimate truth. *Can You Drink the Cup?* was a personal, artistic treatment of a complex theological issue.

Because Henri's approach was artistic, and not that of a scribe or a scholar, it required a special sensibility. He had to focus on the real essence of things. Because he was so focused on what was real, Henri's approach reminded many people of the approach taken by Jesus. Jesus also recast everything, and Jesus "did not speak as the scribes," either. However, I don't think Henri was necessarily trying to follow the example of Jesus in his way of interpreting things. The origins of his special approach are more complex.

I want to explore the origins and expression of Nouwen's way of understanding life and the gospel now, because if there is one thing that I wish we could learn or absorb from Henri Nouwen, it is the contemplative, full-bodied embrace of life that emerged from his blending of faith and creativity. I myself have studied contemplative spirituality for most of my adult life, but I have found few examples of the lively originality and passionate embrace of God and of the world that I find in Henri. I think it was inspired by God, but I also suspect it was inspired by Vincent van Gogh and a few others, so let us ask how this wonderful talent developed.

Vincent

Vincent van Gogh was indeed a great source of inspiration for Henri Nouwen. At this writing it appears that he has become the world's favorite painter as well. Wherever one looks today there are posters, calendars, and books celebrating the art of this uniquely talented man who signed his paintings simply as "Vincent." Paradoxically, after living a troubled and lonely life, Vincent van Gogh has become the most popular artist in the world. Henri became interested in Vincent before he became quite the star he is today, and the course Nouwen taught on van Gogh at Yale University was thought by many to have been Nouwen's best.[12]

There were a number of parallels in the lives of the painter and the priest. Of course, both were Dutchmen. Both experienced great emotional trials and both struggled with feelings of shame and rejection. Both also answered an early call to religious service. As in Henri's case, when Vincent was a young man, religion was his first priority. He embarked on a preaching mission to the poor working in the mines of Great Britain. Later he went through a mystical period when meditation on scripture became his mainstay. Both of these spiritual experiences in Vincent's life have parallels in the life of the young Henri Nouwen. Henri even went on a mission to the mines of south Limburg.[13]

Both men also struggled with their fathers, who hoped that their sons would make something of themselves. Vincent's father was a Calvinist pastor, a position that was highly respected in Dutch society. He wanted to see Vincent take part in some prosperous business venture. Although Henri's choice to be a priest was never questioned by his father, he suffered all his life with feelings that he could not do enough to earn his father's respect and that all he had accomplished was insufficient in his father's eyes.

The pattern of the two lives begins to diverge as Vincent starts moving beyond Holland. Vincent needed to find a way to escape the disciplined but uninspired mindset and lifestyle that can be typical of northern Europe. To this end, he began to pay more and more attention to what was happening in France. In that country he discovered a way of living that was more passionate, more communal, and in every way brighter than life in the north and, for him, this was a critically important step.

The attraction to France had begun with Vincent's reading of the yellow, paper-bound novels of writers such as Victor Hugo, an author who combined a belief in the virtue of the poor and downtrodden with an awakening to the romance of living more fully. Hugo is an idealistic and exuberant writer, who says, in his *Les Misérables*, "To love another person is to see the face of God." At that time, and especially in Holland, such a claim was quite controversial. Yellow-backed novels from France in general symbolized decadence and impropriety to the conservative-minded Dutch, and Vincent read them almost as an act of protest.

By reading these novels and by following other currents in French thinking, Vincent discovered a way forward that was also a way downward. To reach God, he declared to his brother, one need not be in a seminary. One could study Rembrandt, or the French Revolution or simply be part of the "great university of misery."[14] His feelings solidified, and the death of Vincent's father led to a declaration by the son of how things stood: Vincent expressed his feelings through a painting that reveals the spiritual crossroads at which he had arrived: *Still Life with Open Bible and Zola Novel* shows his father's large Bible propped open to Isaiah 53, the celebrated passage on the Suffering Servant.

Here, for Vincent, was the heart of scripture—an afflicted and cast-off figure suffers in misery and yet bears God's promise! The mystery of God is found revealed through the poor and the meek, even the despised. Beside his father's Bible stands a candle, but the wick is snuffed out. This seems to mean that his father's life and his father's way have ended. It is not difficult to see that Vincent is trying in this painting to show his father, even after his death, where to find the true meaning of scripture. For Vincent, this was a cherished desire, one he had had for some time. He had often hoped to make his father see things his way, as he once wrote to his brother Theo:

> I do not consider Father an enemy, but a friend who would be even more my friend if he were less afraid that I might "infect" him with French "errors." I think if Father understood my real intentions, I could often be some use to him, even with his sermons, because I sometimes see a text in quite a different light. But Father thinks my opinion entirely wrong, considers it contraband, and systematically rejects it.[15]

In a final dramatic stroke, Vincent places in *Still Life* alongside the open Bible an object that his father would have found quite alien to it, a yellow French paperback, and a recent one at that. The book is Zola's *La Joie de vivre*. Perhaps the title itself expresses the one element that Vincent found most lacking in Dutch Calvinism—the joy of life—but the novel's plot is even more telling. In *La Joie de vivre* Zola recounts the life of a miserable bourgeois family reduced to bickering among themselves and the other villagers. A shining heroine appears in the person of an orphaned woman who comes to live with the family and, through her virtue and self-sacrifice, she brings light to their dark world. By positioning Zola's novel alongside the Bible, Vincent is saying that there is virtue and truth everywhere, both in and out of the Bible, and in and out of respectable society. This was Hugo and Zola's creed, and it would be Vincent's creed, too.

The pull of French thinking and art led Vincent and his brother Theo to Paris, and there Vincent found kindred spirits among the Impressionist school of artists. The phenomenal art that Vincent produced while living in France and that later enraptured the world was his way of communing with his adopted culture, a culture that celebrated life through music, wine, wonderful cuisine, and of course painting and other forms of art. Not only was France as a country more open and alive artistically and philosophically than Holland, it was also a society that did not hold the poor and the ordinary people of the farms and the streets in contempt. This was especially important to van Gogh. Although Vincent was a troubled man to the end of his days, in France he found a place where he was more comfortable and where he could embrace life to the fullest extent possible.

Did Henri Nouwen have a similar need to get out of Holland and embrace a more vibrant culture? He certainly followed a pathway out of Holland, and his absence during the social upheavals that began in 1968 left him feeling alienated from his homeland for a certain period. However, Nouwen never broke with Holland. He maintained important friendships with numerous individuals there, not to mention his strong family ties. Even as his international, English-language ministry grew, he continued to speak and write pieces for his Dutch-language audience. He maintained control of the translation and publication of his books in Dutch and he never sought to change his nationality or his allegiance to his Dutch bishop. Holland remained his home.

However, he didn't live there. Clearly, the country—other than Holland—that influenced Henri the most was the United States. He came to feel extremely comfortable on the other side of the Atlantic, even if he never stopped being a Dutchman.

Henri's simple books and his dramatic and exclamatory style of speaking fit the United States much better than it did Europe. He did not like to think that his style was "Americanized," however. Once he spoke before an Eastern European group that clearly did not buy what he was saying. When he heard afterwards that they found his presentation "too American," he replied pointedly, "Maybe it was just too Henri Nouwen!" Henri was very Dutch and very much at home in the United States, at the same time and with very little conflict. Moving to Toronto was in many ways a stroke of genius for Nouwen, because, culturally, Canada stands halfway between the United States and Britain or Europe.

There is such a strong "joie de vivre" element in Henri's life and ministry that I wonder if he himself may have read a few yellow novels by Victor Hugo in his youth like Vincent did. Henri spoke French, although not very fluently, and he probably always had an idea of what France stands for. I imagine that the French theological currents moving through Holland prior to Vatican II were probably the first strong taste he had of that culture. As a seminarian Henri would have realized that the experiments taking place in Holland were part of a theology born in France. The art of Vincent van Gogh eventually became another avenue by which the more artistic and tolerant French sensibility made its way to Henri Nouwen. While at Yale and looking for a new and better way of living, Henri gravitated toward Thomas Merton, who was born in France and whose mother was a lifelong Francophile, and then to the Cistercians, a French monastic order. All in all, that is more than a bit of French influence.

The greatest exponent of French sensibility in Henri's life came to him late, in the form of l'Arche. Although l'Arche today conceives of itself more and more in international and ecumenical terms, its origins are marked by the spirit of French Catholicism. In 1985, when Henri Nouwen visited l'Arche in Trosly, in the countryside near Paris, he was deeply affected by what he saw and experienced, and his life immediately began to change.

L'Arche is a spiritual phenomenon and gift to the world that cannot be characterized as a mere cultural expression. However, in the care given to the small and vulnerable aspects of life, in the joy and the endless celebrations of birthdays and holidays, and even in its sacramentality, l'Arche betrays an especially French sensibility. Some of the same qualities found in l'Arche, the same blend of care and celebration, can also be found in the watercolors of Monet or in a classically prepared meal in a French restaurant. Not everything in France today is peaceful or inspiring, but for Henri Nouwen, a Dutchman living in the fast-paced, pressurized East Coast of the United States, l'Arche and its surroundings provided a welcome respite. There he found and embraced a sweeter, slower, more spiritual and more artistic way of living, just as van Gogh had when he moved to France.

Van Gogh and Nouwen seemed to have been drawn in similar directions, as if they were soul mates. We might picture the two figures as two boats drifting down the same river at different points in time. A religious impulse was fundamental to each of them. Both men were high-strung and wounded, but also phenomenally gifted. They both departed from Holland, thus achieving a broader perspective and embracing a vision that combined concern for the poor with the celebration and love of life, a vision that was nurtured by Latin-spirited France. Having established that there are some interesting parallels between the two men, let us turn to look more carefully at Vincent's art to see what else it may have taught Henri.

When I look at van Gogh's art, at his prosaic subjects painted in swirling colors, and think about Henri, I would begin my comparison by observing that both van Gogh and Nouwen were fascinated by ordinary people and appreciated their humanity. One of van Gogh's most interesting paintings,

The Potato Eaters, shocked its original viewers for its portrayal of peasants living on the dark margins of European culture. Both van Gogh and Nouwen turned their gaze from the privileged world to the world of the poor and of the host of ordinary people in between. Van Gogh was much more aware of nature and landscape than Nouwen, but there is an element of van Gogh's celebration of nature in Nouwen's love of flowers, especially sunflowers, and also in Nouwen's almost Japanese sense of simplicity, composition, and color that is found not only in his writing, but was part of the way Henri said Mass, or decorated his rooms and chapels.

We have seen how Henri Nouwen looked subjectively at the topics before him. Likewise, there never was much realism in Vincent. If van Gogh set himself to paint a peasant toiling beneath the unrelenting heat of the sun, the golden disk might become as huge as the sky itself. The painter "Vincent" did not begin by measuring the proportionate size and height of the sun, or trace its place onto the painting using a grid. He made no attempt to get the scene before him "right" in any empirical sense. Instead, he simply stood in the field and fixed his gaze on the ball of light. As it climbed slowly across the sky, Vincent rose with it in his own spirit. He felt its powerful rays beating down upon field and farmer and glancing off in every direction. He allowed the brilliant light to burn his skin, half blind his eyes, crack his lips, and bring out the sweat on his brow. He would pile vibrant yellow paint onto the surface in gobs and heavy layers in order to transmit some sense of the overpowering intensity of that circle of relentless heat that simmered in the sky above the weary laborers.

What he ultimately painted was not so much a record of what he had seen but a tableau of what he had experienced—it was a meditation on the immensity of the sun's scorching presence, a statement that he took down, not with pen and paper, but inscribed onto canvas with intense colors and light. His study of the sun also became a meditation on the furrowed dirt of the fields, the sunflowers and other vegetation, even on mortal humanity's toil and tenuous place on the earth. He created a great artistic vision, whether his subject was the sky, the water, the earth, or another human being. To every subject he applied the lens of his own intense, artistic temperament. As Henri remarked about van Gogh shortly before he died, "All the people he paints are radiant like saints and his orchids, cypresses and wheat fields are burning with the fire of his intense feelings."[16]

Like El Greco before him, and like Michelangelo in our earlier example, as Vincent worked at his subject, it shifted and changed. A wheat field could take on a deep blue hue, a night sky could break apart like the waves of the sea, and a human face could grow elongated and become etched with purple lines. What emerged was something not so much distorted as transformed. Henri, in like manner, did not merely observe the issues and the people before him, he engaged them contemplatively and creatively. As he took a topic into his hands, it went through a metamorphosis. By owning a topic and working it, Henri also produced the same transformation, the same kind of wider vision we see in the artists like Vincent who were his spiritual companions. They influenced him stylistically and even philosophically. They helped him see the world from below, and in a new and transformed way.

Can we say that Henri Nouwen did for spirituality what Vincent van Gogh did for art? Did Nouwen in fact take spirituality into an Impressionist phase? When one looks at the almost scholastic approach taken to spirituality in the older Catholic manuals, with their formal categories and concern for orthodoxy, one might very well say yes—Henri Nouwen did open a vast new vista, and did so from a personal and artistic viewpoint. Yes, he was like an Impressionist set loose in the library of Christian belief.

Thomas Merton

Henri Nouwen was not alone in what he accomplished, but, then again, neither was Vincent van Gogh. Both men were part of larger movements. There were a number of spiritual writers that Nouwen drew on and who preceded him in the formation of his vision. Probably the writer from whom Henri learned most was Thomas Merton. Merton was a young university intellectual who converted to Catholicism and ultimately became a Cistercian monk. Through a series of remarkable publications on a wide number of topics, Merton brought about a transformation of Christian spirituality. Both Merton and Nouwen were revolutionary writers who advanced creatively through their chosen subjects. Both stood within the bounds of Catholicism looking out at the world around them.

What was most different about Merton was that he was an intellectual, someone who was able to write about politics, philosophy, literature, and culture—to name only a handful of the concerns of this monk who was interested in everything. Henri Nouwen was never that kind of thinker. Henri's focus was ever on the experience of faith. Therefore, it is in relation to Merton's autobiographical works, especially his classic *Seven Storey Mountain*, that Merton and Nouwen are most alike. In Merton we find a figure who is enraptured by a vision of Catholic Christianity as a key to understanding the universe. Like Nouwen, Merton transforms and updates all the topics he addresses. He has the same sense of vivid, living faith as Nouwen, if not Henri's emotional vulnerability and sensitivity.

What Merton said he was engaged in was a kind of contemplative living that was a merging of religious and artistic seeing and understanding. As a contemplative monk, he drew on a range of earlier mystical figures, some of whom he reintroduced to the world. Since his tastes were also very broad, his mental landscape also included poets from Latin America, European philosophers, and Eastern, especially Zen, contemplative masters.[17]

Thomas Merton provided Henri Nouwen with a model of an artist engaged in prayer and spiritual writing. Merton, like van Gogh, epitomized for Henri a kind of engaged contemplation of God in what can be seen before us. One finds in Merton the same preference for a world truly understood, rather than transcended. This means that many times one sees in Merton a world that is perfectly ordinary, not pierced by a miraculous divinity. An epiphany in Merton is sometimes a non-finding. Consider this passage:

> [C]ontemplation is not vision because it sees "without seeing" and knows "without knowing." It is a more profound depth of faith, a knowledge too deep to be grasped in images, in words, or even in clear concepts. It can be suggested by words, by symbols, but in the very moment of trying to indicate what it knows the contemplative mind takes back what it has said, and denies what it has affirmed. For in contemplation we know by "unknowing." Or better, we know *beyond* all knowing or "unknowing." Poetry, music and art have something in common with the contemplative experience. But contemplation is beyond aesthetic intuition, beyond art, beyond poetry... It knows God by seeming to touch Him. Or rather it knows Him as if it had been invisibly touched by Him... Touched by Him who has no hands, but who is pure Reality and the source of all that is real! Hence, contemplation is a sudden gift of awareness, an awakening to the Real within all that is real.[18]

Nouwen delighted in the way in which Merton took apart a problem and discarded as inessential most of what we see, and he was convinced that Merton was right in focusing on the world as we find it, rather than what is beyond the world. To find the world we must begin in the world and strip away the husk until we find the perfectly pure kernel at the center. Listen to what Nouwen once observed about Merton's ability to see God at work:

> We are called to be contemplatives, that is *see-ers*, men and women who are called to see the coming of God. The day of the Lord is indeed always coming. It is not a coming which will occur in some distant future, but a coming here and now among us. The Lord's coming is an ongoing event around us, between us, and within us. To become a contemplative, therefore, means to throw off—or better, to peel off—the blindfolds that prevent us from *seeing* his coming in the midst of our own world. Like John the Baptist, Merton constantly points away from himself to the coming One, and invites us to purify our hearts so that we might indeed recognize him as our Lord... Thomas Merton invites us to an always deeper awareness of the incomprehensibility of God. He continually unmasks the illusions that we know God and so frees us to see the Lord in always new and surprising ways.[19]

Becoming free to see things in "new and surprising ways" was central to the vocations of Thomas Merton, Vincent van Gogh, and Henri Nouwen, and the type of "seeing" they practiced proceeds from a similar kind of contemplative and artistic engagement. This creative process leads to a deeper comprehension of aspects of the world that are normally hidden or unnoticed. One can even say that it ultimately points toward deeper realities beyond this world.

Henri took up this legacy of artistic vision, or spirit, and of writing his way into God. I will never forget arriving to visit him one day and meeting him as he came down the stairway to answer the door. He stopped about ten feet up the stairs from where I was. Still alive with the excitement of what he had been writing, he exclaimed, "I have been working with words!" As I looked up at his joyful face, framed in a halo of uncombed hair, it seemed that he had truly been airborne and only reluctantly had come down for a landing. He had been engaged in his real work, a way of writing that was part prayer, part artistic creation, and part contemplation.

In Nouwen's sort of contemplation, the imagination does not have free reign, nor is there any withdrawal from reality. It was important for Henri that contemplation not be seen as some kind of escapism. Vincent van Gogh, Thomas Merton, and Henri Nouwen were not looking beyond this world in search of some heavenly realm. All three were seeking God's presence in the world around us. This was the reason why Vincent, although a very spiritual man, avoided religious subjects, such as scenes from the Bible. He thought that this was all heady imagination. He wanted to show that God is present by simply painting an olive grove in such a way at to lead the viewer to higher things.[20] Merton and Nouwen held to this principle also.

Henri's way of keeping things real was to avoid intellectualism, and he did not make reference to spiritual authorities or even doctrines. He avoided religious language and references. Indeed, he had surprisingly little interest in some of the classic figures of the Christian spiritual tradition. Although centered on the Bible and the Eucharist, he preferred to explore the ordinary elements of existence and the pathway of his own feelings. Henri had a special gift for taking up familiar aspects of religion and of ordinary living and making them come alive. Words that we all know by heart, stories we have heard countless times, truths that we repeat or recite but that have grown stale and remote—he could infuse with new meaning. This ability to make familiar things come alive was the fruit of his creative, contemplative process of living in the world. Henri's spirituality was intimately bound up in personal artistic contemplation, and, as a preacher or writer, he wove words around whatever event or story or image he was considering.

What we might learn from this? I think that learning to see the world in this new way is a task that could certainly take most of a lifetime. What van Gogh, Merton, and especially Nouwen were doing was contemplation—van Gogh before a landscape, Merton before a Zen koan, and Nouwen before the biblical image of the Prodigal Son—but that contemplation became art because of each individual's creative propensity and power. All became witnesses, recording what they saw, staring intently until the outlines blurred. To engage in their practice, one must dwell deeply, repetitively yet creatively, with an idea, an image, or a feeling until, after a time, that idea or image blossoms within oneself into a new and liberating vision.

If we are to claim this piece of the Nouwen legacy, it will not be by being faithful to the same topics or the same approach as Henri's, but by ourselves becoming artists and living our lives in faithful openness to the vision of God and the world. Henri had those who taught him how to see, such as Rembrandt, or van Gogh, or Boisen, or Merton. We must choose our own guides, our own artists, our own authors, and allow the seeds of their vision to flower in the soil of our lives. I suppose that what Nouwen has left for us, more than anything else, is an invitation to join in the rich and living tradition to which he belonged. Whether we turn ultimately to the piano, to the painter's easel, to the garden, to the writer's notebook, or to offer our lives in service, we will carry forward the bright vision, the special awareness, of the world as Henri taught us to see it, a world not to be transcended but to be embraced by those truly alive.

4

EATING AND DRINKING
IN THE HOUSE OF GOD

The Culture of the Eucharist

Large rivers like the Nile, the Ganges, the Mississippi, and the Amazon support and nourish the lands through which they flow. In the same way, one can say that the Eucharist gave shape to and sustained the rich life and work of Henri Nouwen. The spiritual meal of the Christian Church coursed through his existence, carving a wide channel. Like a large and mighty river, it flowed within and flooded his life with powerful currents that changed him and rearranged his boundaries. Henri's deep absorption in the Eucharist, when combined with his ecumenical ministry, ultimately even took him beyond the norms of Roman Catholicism.

Henri rode the meditative currents of this river to the formation of a new teaching on the Eucharist that recalled the original sense of the meal. Nouwen reminds us that Jesus, by eating and drinking with his disciples before and after his death and resurrection, established a firm friendship with them and with us. At the table of Jesus we are not only welcomed and given food and wine, but we find our individual trials and triumphs held aloft for a toast, blessed and included. Nouwen's simple but profound teaching returns the focus of the Eucharist from the realm of ecclesiastical doctrine and ceremony to Jesus and to the life experience of those gathered around his table.

Nouwen's focus on this sacrament began early. As a child, Henri Nouwen was drawn almost magnetically to the Eucharist. As we have seen, by the time he was eight he had constructed a miniature chapel in the family attic. There he spent long hours, not only delivering sermons to his family and friends, but ruminating on and carefully reenacting the sacred sharing of Christ's blood and body, the high point of the Catholic Mass. The Eucharist undergirded the rest of his life, and it was to the Eucharist that he turned when writing the last book he would see published in his lifetime. This work, entitled *Can You Drink the Cup?*,[1] is a deceptively simple but powerful testimony to a life so wound around a core of eucharistic thinking that the sacred meal and the rest of Nouwen's life blended into one.

In Christianity, the Eucharist is a way to experience God. Participation in the Eucharist has also been an exclusive privilege of membership in Christian communities of faith. The sharing of the bread and the cup signifies entry into communion with another person or with that entire group. Therefore, some Protestants, most Orthodox, and all Catholic Christians are not permitted to participate in the eucharistic life of other denominations. Christians around the world are not as a rule "in communion" one with another. Moreover, individuals who seriously violate the norms of their churches are "excommunicated," which means that they are forbidden to share in that group's Eucharist. The Eucharist is thus a rite both of inclusion and exclusion. It is a powerful symbol, considered by most Christians to contain elements of both awe and divine mystery. In earliest Christianity, the Eucharist was considered so holy that it was performed in private and kept a secret from outsiders. In the sixteenth century Martin Luther is known to have fainted as a young priest at the awesome prospect of celebrating a Mass and handling the body and blood of Christ.

Today the Eucharist still plays the dominant role in the worship of Roman Catholics. It is helpful to remember this when thinking about Henri Nouwen. In Catholicism, the celebration of the Mass has expanded over the centuries to the point that it has eclipsed or replaced many other services and rituals. More than Protestantism, where the Lord's Supper is much less central, and even Eastern Orthodoxy, which has many services that are not eucharistic and which does not practice frequent communion, Roman Catholicism places enormous emphasis on the Mass and on communion.

As a seminarian, Henri Nouwen attended Mass daily and was trained to perform the Eucharist properly according to the Roman rite. Celebrating the Eucharist was really the sign and primary purpose of his priesthood. Presiding at the Eucharist is an exclusive prerogative of the priesthood in Catholicism, and the celebration of the Mass is the basic activity for which Catholics gather together on Sundays. The priest is central to the Mass, and the Mass is central to the faith. Thus Henri Nouwen, by virtue of his priesthood, stood at the center of Christian experience as his community understood it.

The Eucharist is the most common and well known of Catholic practices, but it also has a deeper, more complex side. Lively debates have flourished around the theory and practice of the Eucharist, as have mystical and devotional practices and experiences related to it. Most Christian churches, but particularly the Catholic Church, have precise and even elaborate doctrines detailing the way in which Christ is present in the eucharistic elements. Transubstantiation, consubstantiation, real presence—these are just some of the better known doctrinal concepts that characterize the doctrine of the Eucharist.

Although these official theological developments are important, they are dwarfed by the devotional traditions and mystical practices that have developed around taking communion and venerating the eucharistic elements, meaning the bread and the wine. Many of these are huge public functions. For example, it is common in Catholicism to display the eucharistic host, the wafer of bread, for purposes of contemplation, and it can even be carried in procession through the streets of a city in the more traditional Catholic countries. Henri Nouwen, who attended or presided over Mass daily for most of his life, was in fact steeped in a rich eucharistic culture that was not of his making; it was a central aspect of the inherited tradition of Catholicism.

It is against this background, this eucharistic culture, that the brilliant creativity and meaning of Nouwen's eucharistic practice and vision should be assessed. Both Nouwen's way of celebrating the Eucharist and his spiritual writings regarding it were departures from the Catholic norm. How were they different? Very briefly, I would say that Henri Nouwen did not approach the Eucharist as a familiar and hallowed tradition, in the way common to most Catholics. Instead, he presented it as a vital aspect of the life and ministry of Jesus, as a moment when Jesus reaches out and invites everyone to join him at the table.

Learning from the Disabled

Over the years that I knew him, I watched Henri Nouwen say Mass many times in a number of different settings—in university chapels, in churches, and in private homes. Being present at one of Henri's Masses was always a special occasion, but I believe that by the last years of his life his way of celebrating Mass had evolved into something even more meaningful than it had been previously. I think this change was partly due to the presence of the handicapped at his services at Daybreak and elsewhere. The handicapped helped Henri and everyone else to slow down and consider what they were doing. What emerged for Henri and for his community in that period was a special insight, or a heightened awareness regarding the presence of Jesus in the Eucharist.

When Henri Nouwen presided over a Mass at Dayspring chapel, as his Daybreak retreat and residence was called, he sat at a low altar so as to not separate himself from others or raise himself above them. This is something he had begun to do years earlier. He also wore rich vestments in order to reach even the profoundly retarded with a bright color or a sense of happy celebration. Many of the physically disabled sat or were held on beanbags because their deformities or conditions did not permit them to sit on chairs. In these years, Henri's path through the service became slow and deliberate. In fact, it seemed like he was enacting a special meditation over each ritual. He put so much feeling into every word and gesture that it seemed as if one were watching Jesus say for the very first time, "Take, eat, this is my body which is given up for you."

Breathing in the incense, soaking up the readings, and watching Henri's slow, carefully dramatized movements made me feel like I had arrived at some deeper, richer understanding of the gospel. Henri himself said of these Masses with the handicapped:

> It is the presence of Jesus among us, real and concrete, that gives us hope. It is eating and drinking here that creates the desire for the heavenly banquet, it is finding a home now that makes us long for the father's house with its many dwelling places. Who better than severely mentally handicapped people can teach us this liberating truth? They do not read newspapers, watch

television, or discuss the possibilities of a future disaster. They do not dwell upon the future. Instead they say, "Feed me, dress me, touch me, hold me...Kiss me, speak to me. It is good to be here together now."[2]

This sense of "being in the present," both mentally and physically, was transmitted to everyone present by l'Arche core members. Henri not only received from the handicapped this gift of a slower, more meditative Eucharist, he put it into practice when he said Mass elsewhere. I will always remember the last Mass I went to at Daybreak while Henri was alive. My wife and I had gone to Toronto to visit Henri, and we had even dared to accept his invitation that we take our five-year-old twin boys along on the trip. Over the course of three days Henri was the perfect, generous host to our family. He had even laid in a small supply of borrowed toys in preparation for the boys' visit. He had never had a family stay with him before, so we were a challenge to his hospitality. However, everything went well. It was a wonderful visit, one that constituted a unique moment in our friendship.

Our last day there happened to be Palm Sunday. Since we would be flying out by midmorning, Marta and I woke up early and went downstairs to Henri's first Mass. Somehow our movements must have woken our boys, because they both appeared minutes later in the chapel, still in pajamas and half asleep. Andrés was in tears because he assumed we had left for the airport without them! Seeing that we were still there, he calmed down and curled up on my lap. Nicolás lay down on a bean bag near Marta.

They quietly followed the Palm Sunday readings, which told of Jesus entering Jerusalem on a donkey. Then, when Henri was in the middle of the sermon, Nicolás suddenly blurted out a question:

"Why didn't Jesus ride a horse?" Henri paused in what he was saying and pondered this with both boys, just as he had worked through similar questions during meals and while telling bedtime stories during the last several days. From the five-year-old perspective, this question was an important element of the story. The three of them decided that horses are for rich people, and Jesus was only a poor man, so riding a donkey was the right thing for him to do.

Later, when it came time for the presentation of the gifts, Henri called the boys to his side. Under his supervision they proudly poured the wine into tall glass goblets. Then they watched Henri's consecration with rapt attention. We all did. For that moment, the world stood still. The low altar was heaped with palm fronds, the candles flickered, the handicapped shifted and moaned in the half darkness, and we able-bodied adults smiled and bowed our heads as we faced the priest flanked by two little boys in sleeper pajamas. Jesus was a poor man and had been a friend to little people like these—and broken people like us. Hosanna in the highest.

Keeping it Simple

Watching Henri Nouwen preside over the Eucharist, one was continually struck by the immediacy and dramatic intensity that he brought to the ritual. The depth of expression and feeling was fresh and arresting, not formal, routine, or regurgitated. In addition, he made the eucharistic celebration an extension of his preaching. Just as he reached out, drawing in and convincing his audience while preaching, he also made the assembled congregation part of his celebration of the Eucharist. He included them, whoever they might be. Around him might be a young family, as we had been that day, or it might be jaded Catholic observers or puzzled Protestants or even alienated outsiders. To reach even people with little understanding of the Eucharist, Nouwen began with Jesus himself, and never strayed from this focus. As he presented it, the Eucharist was a moment of friendship and intimacy shared between Jesus and his friends, whether at the Last Supper, on the road to Emmaus, or right now, at this very moment. His attitude comes through clearly in *With Burning Hearts*,

> "Now while he was with them at table, he took the bread and said the blessing; then he broke it and handed it to them." So simple, so ordinary, so obvious, and still—so very different! What else can you do when you share bread with your friends? You take it, bless it, break it and give it. That is what bread is for: to be taken, blessed, broken and given. Nothing new, nothing surprising. It happens every day, in countless homes. It belongs to the essence of living. We can't really live without bread that is taken, blessed, broken and given. Without it there is no table fellowship, no community, no bond of friendship, no peace, no love, no hope. Yet with it, all can become new!
>
> Maybe we have forgotten that the Eucharist is a simple human gesture . . . Every time we invite Jesus into our homes, that is to say, into our life with all its light and dark sides, and offer him the place of honor at our table, he takes the bread and the cup and hands them to us, saying: "Take and eat, this is my body. Take and drink, this is my blood. Do this to remember me."[3]

With words such as these, as Henri lifted the bread and wine and shared them, he transported everyone taking part into that original circle of communion around Jesus. Any formal surroundings or the importance of ritual and tradition were forgotten. Henri's deeply felt eucharistic celebration was just that—a celebration! It was so vibrant and unconventional by Catholic standards that it almost felt like an evangelical service, especially because of Henri's emphasis on Jesus. Yet how could it not also be Catholic—deeply Catholic—for a priest to move the focus of the Eucharist back to Jesus, reciting carefully the words from the missal heard every Sunday?

In the end, both Protestants and Catholics felt included and completely at home around Henri Nouwen's altar, and everyone communicated. In the midst of such a moving experience, such an evocation of Jesus as the one welcoming everyone to the table, not taking part would have been hard, almost a sin against the Spirit.

Seeing a New Unity

Intercommunion thus became the principal area in which Nouwen went beyond the limits of Roman Catholic practice. This change took place not at l'Arche, but much earlier, and there are probably several reasons why he deviated from a clear rule that Roman Catholics everywhere adhere to. In the turbulent period of the sixties, when Nouwen was a professor and de facto chaplain at Yale Divinity School, an ecumenical—but chiefly Protestant—institution, the Masses he celebrated in the chapel of the Yale Divinity School became a staple of that theological community's life and a major part of his ministry there. Protestant students were attracted to his Masses and began to take regular part in them. It was, after all, an ecumenical chapel. When Nouwen was absent, an Episcopal priest performed an Episcopal service. Since Henri Nouwen had been trained and ordained during a period of great liturgical experimentation and reform in Holland, the inclusion of Protestants in the circle of communion at Yale must have seemed to him like a permissible next step forward. Given the circumstances, it may have even seemed unavoidable to him.

By this point, it was Catholic policy not to turn anyone away from communion except notorious sinners, and many, if not most of the firm rules from the pre-Vatican II past seemed to be enforced less and less. It was a time of freedom and upheaval, and Nouwen would have felt even less restraint than other Catholic priests. Not only was he employed in a Protestant institution, his own bishop was in Holland and he was not formally tied to any American diocese or religious order. Thus, he enjoyed an unusual degree of freedom from regulation and scrutiny for a Catholic priest. We have a testimonial from one of his Protestant students at Yale that she posted on an Internet website:

> I met Henri when I was a student at Yale—I wouldn't consider myself close—but when I was in a low state spiritually I started to attend the small mass he conducted Monday through Thursday in the crypt chapel. He didn't say Mass on Friday because that was the community service—his sense of community and ecumenical oneness overcame any exclusivity. And so I attended his mass right before dinner, even though I was not a Roman Catholic. And when I declined communion he asked me later why—and I said I wasn't a Roman Catholic—and he said—Oh, that's nothing! So I was part of the community to him. Henri taught me about the Eucharist and it's significance in a hurting world. And I have never forgotten that lesson.[4]

I realize that some persons will be disappointed in Henri Nouwen or think less of him because he did not follow a rule that they feel is like a bright line dividing Catholicism from Protestantism. It is true that Henri Nouwen was willing to break rules, but, like Jesus, he had a knack for breaking them for just the right reason, that is, he broke rules in order to adhere to a higher rule. Jesus scandalized others when he healed on the Sabbath, and he then explained that human beings were more important than the days of the week. Henri many times went right around the rules as well, as long as a greater truth was served. Henri taught us that the Eucharist is for all Christians, and that it is too important an experience for anyone to be excluded. This is roughly the Catholic position on the rite of baptism, and Nouwen simply extended it to communion.

Later, when his books began to be read more widely and he became well known and popular in Protestant just as much as Catholic circles, the scope of his ministry grew and became even more clearly ecumenical. He eventually realized that he was called to serve all communities and address all Christians. As his work expanded among Protestants, Nouwen also discovered the commonality of Christian experience. He found the same virtues, the same weaknesses, and the same depth of faith in Protestants as he did among Catholic students and listeners. He realized that Catholics were not better Christians than Protestants. Practicing intercommunion in his services did not cause the sky to fall, either. Rather, it demonstrated the truth of what Paul had written long ago, "all are one in Christ Jesus" (Galatians 3:28). As this truth became more and more evident to Nouwen over the course of many years, and as the great natural generosity of his spirit led him to embrace more and more people with an ever-wider range of backgrounds, he became a convinced believer in a new ecumenism, one that not only brought people together but succeeded in making Protestantism and Catholicism more compatible and mutually illuminating.

Nevertheless, ecumenism is a vexed issue, even today. Many theologians express displeasure at the dilution of either Catholicism or Protestantism by "alien" influences from the other side of the divide. Arguments among either type of Christian can be won or lost by claiming that someone is taking things in a too Protestant or too Catholic direction. However, it is a fact that by reading the same authors, listening to the same music, studying in the same schools, and living in the same society, Protestant and Catholic Christians increasingly think alike and embrace each other as brethren.

No one was quicker to understand this than Henri Nouwen. As a priest completely confident of his Catholicism and yet detached from local religious sensibilities because he was living outside his own country, Henri became a Catholic bridge to Protestant America. He was never threatened by Protestant attitudes, and he treated all people as guests and inquirers. His friendly generosity of spirit carried him forward and he learned from everyone. His world was, after all, made up largely of Protestants. The pastoral counseling movement that he became part of early on was almost completely Protestant, as was the Civil Rights movement, as was Yale Divinity School. Protestantism was everywhere he looked.

To this Protestant field of ministry to which he seemed called, Henri Nouwen added not only his own colorful personality, but the yeast of Catholic sacramentalism, the chaste earthiness and depth of its monasticism, its celibacy, and the best aspects of Catholicism's wider and deeper spirituality. Catholicism has a more natural connection to literature, the arts, philosophy, and history than Protestantism. Plus, it has the festivals, the cult of the saints, and a wonderful interface with many different cultures. Henri Nouwen found among his new Protestant friends a deep interest and even a hunger for all these things.

What took place at Nouwen's eucharistic celebrations was thus more than just a Catholic Mass where Protestants were present. As the ministry of this remarkable man unfolded, a deep reconciliation was taking place between two spiritual communities. Through Henri Nouwen and others like him, Christ was drawing his divided household back to one table. I find it significant that two of Henri Nouwen's most trusted and admired friends—Fred Rogers, the "Mr. Rogers" of children's television, and Jean Vanier, the founder of l'Arche—both remarked on Henri's great contribution in the area of ecumenism around a shared Eucharist.[5] These are Jean Vanier's words:

> Henri found his fullness in the Eucharist. He loved to celebrate the Eucharist and to include everybody in it, and if he sometimes seemed a bit casual with the rules of the Roman Catholic Church concerning intercommunion, it was because he wanted each one present to have a personal encounter with Jesus. Henri loved the Eucharist because he loved Jesus. And he believed passionately in the real presence of Jesus in the consecrated bread and wine. Because the Eucharist was of such great significance to him, he had the natural talent for making it meaningful, for showing its connectedness to our lives. He would circle the altar, walk out amongst the participants waving his hands here and there. Some people might have found these actions disturbing but they were all expressions of Henri's intense desire to bring people together, around Jesus... [H]e had the charisma of a unifier. He chose to downplay differences, to overlook contradictions; he preferred cutting to the heart of situations and of people, finding there a deeper unity. By awakening hearts, helping people of different traditions to walk in their inner journeys, to meet Jesus, to rediscover trust in themselves, in their own creativity and intuition, Henri was amongst the great ecumenists of this century.[6]

Nouwen was an ecumenist. He brought the people around him into one body, not by theological argument or by any overt means or manipulation, but simply by keeping his ministry on a personal level. As Jean Vanier said above, he "cut to the heart of situations and people." These words are very significant. In science, and especially in mathematics, the most admired and acclaimed theorems are both elegant and simple. As with $E = mc^2$, some of our biggest mysteries have been resolved into the shortest equations.

However, the ability to see things in simple terms is apparently rare. It does involve cutting to the heart of situations and people. This is another quality that we must credit to Henri Nouwen's ledger. He was able to give us a new teaching on the Eucharist by staying clear of almost everything that had been said during the previous two thousand years and returning to the idea that, in the Eucharist, Jesus is lifting a glass and breaking bread with us, his friends, and exploring all that that means. The Eucharist is part of God's love and friendship with the world. Henri Nouwen arrived at a teaching that his handicapped friends could understand and that also could reach those with a deep familiarity with the Eucharist and revitalize their faith as well.

Finding Our Home in God

Although the Eucharist is a ritual that stands at the very center of Christianity and of the experience of Jesus, it has become so top heavy—not to say overgrown—with formalities that it makes Jesus seem more distant, not more familiar. Furthermore, it has been dulled by ritualization and repetition. It has lost its simplicity. So Henri would need to remind us: "Maybe we have forgotten that the Eucharist is a simple human gesture. The vestments, the candles, the altar servers, the large books, the outstretched arms, the large altar, the songs, the people—nothing seems very simple, very ordinary, very obvious. We often need a booklet to follow the ceremony and understand its meaning."[7]

Meaning is obscured rather than revealed by the layers upon layers of refinement that the centuries have added. For Nouwen, now, in order to find God, we must return to what is simple and ordinary, because that is where God is unexpectedly to be found. This is the paradox, as he writes:

> The Eucharist is the most ordinary and the most divine gesture imaginable. That is the truth of Jesus. So human, yet so divine; so familiar, yet so mysterious; close, yet so revealing!...It is the story of the God who wants to come close to us, so close that we can see him with our own eyes, touch him with our own hands; so close that there is nothing between us and him, nothing that separates, nothing that divides, nothing that creates distance.[8]

Nouwen's teaching on the Eucharist, then, in a nutshell, was this: the Eucharist is a thanksgiving celebration of life. We must see it both in its simplicity and humanity as well as its divine transcendence. As a simple human gesture, it draws together all of humanity, all of our toil, and even the tragedy we encounter here on the face of the earth. All people everywhere go daily to their own tables, to their own families and friends, to share food and drink. We also welcome friends and strangers, celebrate and settle our differences around our tables. It is by sitting and eating together that our lives are reflected fully and have their greatest meaning. The table signifies reconciliation and understanding. The table is a sign of our communion, of our sharing of life with the world and its inhabitants. Those who sit around us and share our food help us to appreciate our humanity and our experience of life. Once we have shared our table with others, we are forever closer to them. Our relationship has changed by our sharing with them an ancient rite of intimacy.

The table where Jesus presides is very much like our own tables. Jesus also greets us there as friends and provides the food and drink which sustain us and form the basis of our fellowship. By eating and drinking together, we enter into a new type of relationship and have greater intimacy with Jesus and with God. We let down our guard, and he does the same. In this simple experience we are reconciled, not only with Jesus, but with all who have been called to the table of God. The bread and the wine, being the "fruit of the vine and work of human hands," extend that reconciliation and sense of oneness further, bringing together the toil and the factuality, the material reality, of all of creation. Creation is gathered up and newly blessed every time the bread and wine are lifted from the table in thanks. We ourselves are gathered up, with our own triumphs and sorrows, our own misgivings and hopes. The Eucharist is both an exploration and a celebration of our lives; it is the place where we take stock and take comfort.

The personal dimension of this sacrament is so easily forgotten. The Mass has so reinforced the communal and institutional character of the Eucharist that we no longer feel that our own lives are involved or reflected in it. Nouwen restores the balance: as we sit at the table, as we lift the cup, we work our way from resentment and alienation to participation and gratitude. This is a personal journey; it is an individual journey. Each of us has our own cup to drink, our own life to live, our own road to travel. The Eucharist can and should be a vehicle for our own unfolding spiritual and personal experience. Before we bless the cup, we hold it up and think about who we are and what God is asking of us. The contents of your cup are your life, your unique situation. Whether we can accept our lot, fully live our life, and find meaning in it are all reflected in Jesus' question, "Can you drink the cup?"

Nouwen's simple but remarkable teaching has brought thousands of Christians closer to God and to a new appreciation of the Eucharist. It is an attractive teaching that few find objection-able. When objections arose that Henri Nouwen was not in com-pliance with Catholic teaching, and they did arise, he pointed out the latitude permitted within canon law for priests to make adap-tations to special pastoral situations. Intercommunion was of course not something Henri Nouwen actually promoted or rec-ommended. Intercommunion was simply something that readily happened in the mixed groups of Christians that he addressed in his years of ministry. When asked about Protestants taking com-munion at Daybreak, he would tell the local bishop in Toronto that handicapped people cannot tell the difference between a Protestant a Catholic, thus pastoral adaptation was required!

Over time, Henri became more and more comfortable with his position in the vanguard of an emerging shared Christian-ity. In his quiet way he did more to make a shared faith a reality than any number of theological delegations formed to bring about closer ties with "separated brethren," mostly because, in the end, for Henri Nouwen there probably was no such thing as a separated brother or sister. Everyone was welcome in his life and at God's table.

5

JESUS AT THE CENTER

A New Teaching

One might ask: Is there any one element in Henri Nouwen's life and teaching that completes the picture, that perhaps even makes up for all of the deficits that might be ascribed to him? The answer to that question is yes—Henri's abiding faith in Jesus, and what he experienced and taught others about Jesus, the Lord. In this regard, his life shows not only insight and creativity but also Henri's charism or giftedness. Henri brought Jesus closer to many, many people. His Protestant readers were attracted to him precisely because they sensed the depth of his faith in Jesus Christ. Senator Mark Hatfield, a Nouwen fan, was one such reader:

> I was in the bookstore in Portland, spending a Saturday afternoon leafing through scores of Christian books, when one book riveted my attention. The author of this book was speaking about the Lord in such intimate and affectionate terms that the person of Jesus Christ jumped out from the book at me and embraced me with warm and enfolding arms. My curiosity knew no

bounds: who was this author, this Henri Nouwen, who spoke of our Lord with such color and candor?[1]

Henri Nouwen did indeed walk in the company of the man from Nazareth, and the lifelong journey they undertook together had all the dynamics and nuances of a real friendship. Their relationship was not always perfectly harmonious. I think that Henri was sometimes surprised that Jesus did not reveal himself more clearly to him. Once Henri wrote:

> My whole life has been an arduous attempt to follow Jesus as I had come to know him through my parents, friends, and teachers. I had spent countless hours studying the Scriptures, listening to lectures and sermons, and reading spiritual books. Jesus had been very close to me, but also very distant; a friend, but also a stranger; a source of hope, but also of fear, guilt and shame.[2]

This passage has the ring of truth to it, for here Henri dares to make clear that a relationship with Jesus is not always easy or a source of joy, just as can be said of any true friendship. Nouwen himself was not always perfectly faithful, either. He tells us that there was a time when he felt that a number of other interests and concerns had crowded out his original focus on Jesus. However, looking back, he could see that Jesus was always there, and, in fact, was right at the center again:

> In every phase of my search I've discovered also that Jesus Christ stands at the center of my seeking. If you were to ask me point-blank, "What does it mean to you to live spiritually?" I would have to reply, "Living with Jesus at the center." Countless questions, problems, discussions, and difficulties always demand one's attention. Despite this, when I look back over the last thirty

years of my life, I can say that, for me, the person of
Jesus has come to be more and more important. Increasingly, what matters is getting to know Jesus and
living in solidarity with him. At one time I was so immersed in problems of church and society that my
whole life had become a sort of drawn-out, wearisome
discussion. Jesus had been pushed into the background;
he had himself become just another problem. Fortu-
nately, it hasn't stayed that way. Jesus has stepped out in
front again and asked me, "And you, who do you say
that I am?" It has become clearer to me than ever that
my personal relationship with Jesus is the heart of my
existence.[3]

Henri Nouwen *did* have a life centered on Jesus. His relationship with Jesus may have suffered ups and downs and even
became frayed at times because of neglect or feelings of disappointment, but it remained solid at its core and it increased in vitality. As he matured, Henri found himself thinking and writing
more about Jesus, and he ended up saying some rather important things about Jesus that no one had ever said before. I believe
that just as we all can learn something of great importance from
Henri on the subject of the Eucharist, we can also learn something new from him about Jesus Christ. What was Henri's teaching on Jesus, and how did he come to see Jesus in new ways?

Returning to Jesus

Henri wrote the words that I just quoted in 1985. He was writing in Dutch to his nephew, Marc van Campen. The letters that
he sent to Marc were really quite wonderful, and they ended up
being published as a book, called *Letters to Marc about Jesus*. I
think that correspondence marks the beginning of a turn in

Henri's life back to Jesus, one that would continue to renew itself and bear fruit for the rest of his life. In 1985 Henri was also engaged in a second round of teaching spirituality at Harvard University. I was his assistant, as I had been the previous year.

At that time, as always, there was a whirlwind of activity around Henri, and expectations were running high. For this second year he had been given an independent residence at the divinity school where he would have more space to interact with students and guests. So, in his amazingly openhanded way, he hired a cook and turned his residence into a sanctuary of hospitality and prayer. When he called his assistants in to plan and discuss the course, we would have lengthy sessions, praying in the chapel he had set up and then talking during a big meal we ate together. Henri was creating a real spiritual community at Harvard, and there were always guests at his table.

In addition to the spirituality we were discussing and absorbing, we did have a course to run and administrative issues to deal with. The first problem we faced was class size. We were mobbed with students eager to hear Henri. They came not only from the divinity school but from Harvard College and nearby seminaries and divinity schools. "An Introduction to the Spiritual Life" was the most popular class at the divinity school in living memory. Despite protests, we had to close the class when no one else could squeeze into the largest lecture hall at the divinity school.

As he began to plan out the lectures, Henri told me that this second time around he wanted to do things differently. For one thing, he was shifting from the Gospel of Luke to the Gospel of John. Henri was not given to cryptic remarks, but in this conversation he may have been trying to alert me to the fact that there were some major changes coming.

Whereas Mark and the other gospels build slowly toward acceptance of Jesus as the Messiah, John can seem as blunt and direct as a manifesto. The message of John's gospel goes far beyond the others, becoming both mystical and defiant: "In the beginning was the Word, and the Word was with God, and the Word was God." This is not a subtle or an ambiguous statement. If this opening sentence is true, then Jesus was God *before* his birth, a point that no other gospel makes, especially in such uncompromising terms, and especially not in the very first line. Jesus is presented in John's gospel as a heavenly figure come down to earth. In John's view, acceptance of this "high" Christology was the touchstone of Christian fellowship and faith. Most scholars suppose that this scandalous message was not well received by the Jewish people. The preaching of this message was evidently followed by expulsion of Jewish Christians from synagogues, and this expulsion accounts for the sometimes wounded and bitter tone of the fourth gospel. Although the Gospel of John does sometimes betray a wounded tone, it also presents a profound and soaring vision, not of a sainted Messiah, but of the Son of God come down from heaven.

This unqualified heavenly interpretation of Jesus was rejected by some of John's first-century readers, and it was not going to be an easy sell at Harvard, either. As an institution that is Unitarian in its origins and that draws people from every tradition and every part of the country, Harvard Divinity School gives the appearance of being a model of breadth and tolerance. However, at least in those years, tolerance seldom extended to anyone with strongly articulated mainstream views. To avoid seeming arrogant or triumphalistic, Christianity in particular was not often celebrated at Harvard.

One "down" side of the desire at Harvard to be inclusive and supporting of every minority position was that majority opinions then became suspect. The result was that Harvard Divinity School sometimes could feel like a hothouse environment with a peculiar atmosphere all its own. Many topics that should have been on the agenda were off limits lest someone possibly be offended. Indeed, there were people at Harvard who seemed poised to take offense at anything they deemed insensitive. If you wanted to survive at Harvard, you had to watch what you said around these self-appointed guardians of political correctness.

Henri, as a veteran of the sixties, was no stranger to radical politics or to academic culture, and he had no trouble seeing Harvard Divinity School for what it was. At first Henri took an open and conciliatory stance toward the school's culture of pluralism. He played along with the unspoken restrictions on speech during his first year, but then something changed. He decided to stop mincing words about his Christian convictions. For Henri, Jesus was the center of Christian spirituality, and choosing to focus on the Gospel of John was one way of giving more vocal and unequivocal expression to that fact. During the second year, as Henri became more direct, plain spoken (and powerful, I might add), an inevitable storm of reaction kicked up. Although the students who had come in from the Catholic and evangelical schools and seminaries around Boston rejoiced at what he was saying, a number of Harvard students were indeed offended. Many of them had never heard anyone speak about Jesus with conviction and animation before, and they accused Henri of "spiritual imperialism."

Henri was surprised and distressed by this reaction. Perhaps he had expected his charm and enthusiasm to win everyone over as usual. At one point he asked me, "What *is* spiritual imperialism?" I said that, for the students, it was the worst kind of imperialism, because it used something beautiful—spirituality—in the worst possible way, to dominate and manipulate others. Henri was mystified. This didn't fit his image of himself at all. He had marched with Martin Luther King. He had come to Harvard on the advice of the father of liberation theology, Gustavo Gutiérrez. He thought of himself as a daring ecumenist and a friend of

the poor, but at Harvard he was seen as presumptuous and po-
litically incorrect. He didn't understand that, because he was a
white man representing European culture and Christian belief,
many people at Harvard saw him as part of the problem, not the
solution, and thus he would not be believed when he spoke
about Jesus and the gospel.

Facing rising protests, Henri made some changes to appear
more inclusive, but these gestures appeared superficial. He was
unable to create the harmony he needed in order to feel accepted. His discomfort with the university grew. Things weren't
working. He would write once he left, "I feel no regrets about
my time at Harvard. Though in a divinity school, I had a real
chance to be in a thoroughly secular university environment,
and I had the opportunity to experience joy and fear in speaking
directly about Jesus."[4]

It *was* a time of joy and fear. At Harvard Henri struggled,
sometimes fiercely, with his determination to be true to both
himself and the gospel and with his need to be accepted and
liked. He tried hard to make things work, and it came as a bitter
realization to discover that, despite his reaching out to everyone,
he would not be understood. By the time the class was ending,
Henri was teetering on the edge of serious depression. When he
got like this, he started to doubt everything he was doing.

Henri's decision to opt for Jesus and for his own convictions at Harvard was in fact the visible tip of a looming, still
barely-conscious choice to follow God to deeper levels of Christian experience. He had taken a big risk by leaving his tenured
position at Yale, and he had searched seriously but inconclu-
sively to find a truer expression of his vocation. Now he found
himself suspended midway on the road to some unknown destination. Some days he didn't know if he was going forward or
going crazy. Yet this intense time was as full of light as it was of
darkness. He was opening himself up to greater self-awareness
and even greater changes. This time of crisis also led to deeper

insights into the nature of Christian belief, insights that would show up in his writings years later.

Moving Downward

That last class at Harvard, the apotheosis of his academic career, crystallized some growing insights regarding Jesus. From this point forward, the place of Jesus in Henri's thinking and spirituality only increased. In 1985, John's gospel was helping Henri find words for and a Christian understanding of the strangely inexorable direction his life was taking in the Harvard years, a way that led clearly downward. The gospel also concretized the certainty of rejection. It is in this gospel that Jesus says:

> If the world hates you, you must realize that it hated me before it hated you. If you belonged to the world, the world would love you as its own; but because you do not belong to the world, because my choice of you has drawn you out of the world, that is why the world hates you.[5]

The humiliated Jesus was now making more and more sense to Henri. His own sense of having been rejected—even of failure—was perhaps not a mistake or an accident. It was right in line with the gospel. He felt cast off and unimportant, and yet God was still with him. The road ahead was not going up, but down—down in the sense that Henri was evidently not going to be a Harvard professor or an international peacemaker or much of a public anything, and yet God was still with him...Henri was now in an open field, under the sun where van Gogh had stood, and the gospel of Jesus was changing shape and reforming before his eyes as he worked and lived his life from day to day.

While struggling to know and speak the truth, Henri focused on what he was experiencing and how the gospel could be brought to bear on his life and on the lives of others. There was a new, nakedly secular spirit abroad in the land. Prosperity and making money seemed more important than ever. Some people felt like Jesus was irrelevant to what they were living and that the supposed certainties of the gospel had been shown to be false. Henri was finding the opposite to be true; you just had to see where God was leading. In the Incarnation we see God embarked upon a downward path. There are several points in the gospel where Jesus chooses the way he will go forward, and he invariably makes a choice for humility. Henri had written about this to Marc:

> In the gospel it's quite obvious that Jesus chose the descending way. He chose it not once but over and over again. At each critical moment he deliberately sought the way downwards. Even though at twelve years of age he was already listening to the teachers in the Temple and questioning them, he stayed up to his thirtieth year with his parents in the little-respected town of Nazareth and was submissive to them. Even though Jesus was without sin, he began his public life by joining the ranks of sinners who were being baptized by John in the Jordan. Even though he was full of divine power, he believed that changing stones into bread, seeking popularity, and being counted among the great ones of the earth were temptations.
>
> Again and again you see how Jesus opts for what is small, hidden, and poor, and accordingly declines to wield influence. His many miracles always serve to express his profound compassion with suffering humanity; never are they attempts to call attention to himself. Often he even forbids those he has cured to talk to others

about it. And as Jesus' life continues to unfold, he becomes increasingly aware that he has been called to
fulfill his vocation in suffering and death. In all of this
it becomes plain to us that God has willed to show his
love for the world by descending more and more deeply
into human frailty. In the four accounts of Jesus' life
and death you can see very clearly that the more conscious he becomes of the mission entrusted to him by
the Father, the more he realizes that that mission will
make him poorer and poorer. He has been sent not
only to console poor people, but also to give this consolation as one of them himself. Being poor doesn't just
mean forsaking house and family, becoming a homeless
wanderer, and being increasingly persecuted; it also
means parting company with friends, with success, and
even with the awareness of God's presence. When, finally, Jesus is hanging on the cross and cries out with a
loud voice: "My God, my God, why have you forsaken
me?" only then do we know how far God has gone to
show us his love. For it is then that Jesus has not only
reached his utmost poverty, but also has shown God's
utmost love.[6]

At Harvard, Henri was determined to speak out and identify himself with this Jesus. What the students who misunderstood him failed to realize was that Henri was not proposing an
all-powerful or imperious Jesus, but one who was embarked
upon and called others to this humble, descending way. Henri's
sense of personal connection to the descending Christ was
heightened by the pain he felt at being misunderstood and rejected, but that was not the only reason why this was his focus.
He was also attempting to live out the implications of the considerable time he had spent in Latin America. He had learned
many important lessons there, and had become especially con-

scious of the role the poor of our world must play in any embodiment of the gospel today.

In Latin America he had been fortunate to meet and absorb some of the thinking of a number of inspired liberation theologians, and at Harvard he was trying to transmit some of their insights. I still have a copy of a book Henri gave me that semester. The book was Gustavo Gutiérrez's *We Drink from Our Own Wells*,[7] an exploration of spirituality from the perspective of Latin American poverty. Henri had written the foreword to the English translation of the book. Here was where Henri was finding Jesus.

The meaning of the gospel was also becoming clearer to Henri Nouwen through other new experiences. He was pursuing closer and closer contacts with l'Arche communities, and their unique understanding of the value and mission of the handicapped was also having a profound impact on him. God was indeed calling him to embrace and comprehend more deeply the gospel, but that meant moving downward with Jesus. As Henri searched the gospels for more evidence of this descending way, he realized why it was that Jesus called those who followed him to embrace humility and divest themselves of their own notions or experiences of privilege and power. Like never before in his life, Henri was experiencing more and more solidarity with the poor, and it was all part of identifying with the Christ of the descending way.

These realizations contrasted sharply with the general mood of the society in which he was living. American culture in the mid-eighties was heading in a different direction. These were the Reagan years, and the emergence of "young urban professionals" as a new force in society was being watched with interest. If an earlier generation of young people had been creative or idealistic to a fault, this new group of young people saw themselves as realists with fewer illusions. They wanted the comfort and security that good careers and possessions seemed to offer. Henri was concerned with the seductive power of this "yuppie" mentality and the spiritual poverty to which it could lead, so he took on the somewhat prophetic task of preaching against this trend.

The phrase he seized on to critique this new lifestyle was "upwardly mobile." "Yuppie," like the word "hippie" before it, was a pejorative term that most people would not use to define themselves, but "upwardly mobile" sounded pretty desirable. Who doesn't want to be headed for somewhere better? "Upwardly mobile" sounded optimistic, like "up and coming." It was practically the same as saying someone was headed in the right direction. It sounded like you were beginning with your own life situation and moving ahead, making improvements and looking forward to better things.

Despite his solid middle-class background, Nouwen did not buy into this vision. He warned that such a seemingly straightforward path was not the way in which God's Spirit moves. In fact, worldly recognition and material advancements carry within themselves not merely the seeds of selfishness, but of isolation, jealousy, and doubts that we will ever be loved for who we are, instead of what we have achieved. Instead, Henri taught that God's love is—and our lives should be—a descent and a seeking out of others in the spirit of solidarity with those in need, in pain, and in affliction. This is not upward, but "downward mobility." Going downward means letting go. It means going against not only the expectations of society but also one's own self-interest and desires. It is the way of Christ. It is also the way of humility, the cross, and death. For Nouwen, the Christian, especially the Christian leader, could expect a future in which not even his own self-governance could be taken for granted.[8]

Turning to swim against the stream of normal expectations is not martyrdom, Henri insisted, nor was he suggesting that one should be a psychological weakling when dealing with others. Instead, moving downward is an embrace of a somewhat paradoxical position in which weakness and power are not our own issues, but God's. It is not a negative, life-denying, self-immolation, for, as one descends to a place of solidarity with the lowly, with the poor in spirit, one is touched by an unexpected sense of joy. Jesus was lifted up and, in his resurrection and his ascension, all of those who walk in his steps find themselves transformed and led into new life as well. This is the mystery—one cannot descend with Christ without ascending also. Baptism in fact symbolizes this descent into death and emergence into life, as St. Paul wrote: "[B]y our baptism into his death we were buried with him, so that as Christ was raised from the dead by the Father's glorious power, we should begin living a new life."⁹

As this biblical quotation makes clear, Nouwen's idea about descending with Christ is not actually new. The idea of descending with Christ is central to the New Testament, to monasticism, to the missions, and to a wealth of other Christian expressions throughout the centuries. However, wealth and privilege continue to be prime motivators of a market-driven society that grows larger and more unbalanced over time. Generally, Christians have learned to live with this ambiguity and regard the call to move downward as a saintly option that does not apply to middle-class people struggling to make ends meet.

Therefore it took a special ability or insight and a real desire to be faithful to the gospel for Henri Nouwen to not only present the descending way to those around him but actually begin to live it out. In fact, I would be less interested in Henri Nouwen's teaching about downward mobility and how it relates to Jesus if I had not observed Nouwen practicing what he preached. With Henri Nouwen, it was not merely an idea. Henri's willingness to throw aside concerns about money or his own prestige and his embrace of persons of humbler status was something that I witnessed over and over again.

Living the Gospel

Henri Nouwen's unfeigned humility and lack of concern for his own position or self-interest were a teaching in themselves. He was very open and unguarded. He gave away his books to anyone who crossed his path or wrote to him, constantly sent flowers to all kinds of people and gave money to those in need, even to people who simply had some worthy plan or project. If he thought a sick friend might need a visit to cheer up, he might jump on the next plane and go see him. Henri's remarkable personal generosity was one of his greatest gifts to the world, not only because of the joy he brought into many lives, but because it was such a rare and inspiring expression of freedom.

Since his death, Henri's friends have shared hundreds of stories of his expansive and idealistic behavior, but the anecdote that comes to mind is one told by John Dos Santos, the professor of psychology who had invited Henri to Notre Dame in 1966. He relates a story about picking up Henri at the airport in Mexico City in 1982, when Henri was studying Spanish in Cuernavaca, Mexico. After Nouwen got off the plane from Cuernavaca for his visit with John and his wife, they realized he had nothing with him except the clothes he was wearing. Evidently someone in Cuernavaca had needed help, and Henri had given him his clothes, his money, and everything he had with him.[10] This story impresses me even more than some other tales of Henri's generosity, because keeping one's own comfort zone intact is a high priority when traveling in third-world countries, and even in some parts of Mexico. In the developing world one witnesses real poverty, and the common response is to insulate oneself from it. It is easy to become more hardhearted and less caring. So I am intrigued that Henri had no qualms about giving a stranger everything but the clothes on his back even when he was in Mexico. It sounds like the gospel story about being asked for your shirt and giving your coat as well, and it sounds just like the Henri I knew, too.

Perhaps one of the greater temptations Henri faced in regard to the descending way was the interest shown to him by people in high places. Occasionally it would happen that some fairly famous or wealthy person would find out about Henri and contact him or invite him somewhere. Henri was delighted to occasionally spend time with important or wealthy friends. For example, when Cardinal Bernadin, perhaps the saintliest man in the American hierarchy, was dying and reached out to Henri for spiritual comfort, he felt proud and honored to be asked to advise someone of such integrity.

Henri did enjoy meeting and dealing with important people and visiting nice places. But whereas these sorts of contacts might cause most people's egos to become inflated or their values to slip, this didn't happen very often to Henri Nouwen. Despite the honors, the interest, and the acclaim he received, he somehow remained focused on the descending way, and he was remarkably open to all sorts of people. What he really achieved was an unusual degree of flexibility and lack of prejudice. He spent time with both the humble and the great, yet did not become allied with one kind of person over another.

Of course, the best example of this flexible, more Christian way of living on Nouwen's part was his move from Harvard to l'Arche Daybreak. This was a vast leap downward on his part. He moved from a stimulating intellectual environment, to—as his l'Arche co-worker Sr. Sue Mosteller put it—"this little potato patch, [where he] took up residence with a few people who had mental difficulties, who didn't know he had written a book and couldn't read it if they knew."[11]

If Daybreak was somewhat bleak intellectually, perhaps it was rich in other ways. Going to l'Arche Toronto was the most inspired and perhaps the most inexplicable of the many radical steps Nouwen took in trying to live out the gospel more completely. When he changed his lifestyle from leading classes and participating in university life to caring for handicapped people, he truly embraced his own teaching on downward mobility and he found a group of people that really cared about him, not his achievements.

Since Henri was clueless when it came to many basic practical matters, he had more to learn at l'Arche then a normal person might. He also found it more difficult than most people to gear down and settle into a slow-paced, simple domestic schedule. There was thus a great deal of challenge and psychological growth involved in this transition. Henri was a *puer* type, as we have seen, and the *puer* is naturally a climber and a flyer, driven upward in search of spiritual high points.[12] When Henri's caravan of vehicles pulled up at Daybreak, he was still flying high, but the slower, simpler reality of l'Arche would soon become apparent. Mary Bastedo, part of the leadership team at Daybreak, tells how she viewed Henri's excited arrival:

> Some of us had met Henri during his earlier visit. It was clear that he hardly knew how to make toast and tea, yet he was going to be a house assistant in the New House. Henri had purchased a brand-new car and was driving with his soon-to-be head of house, talking excitedly about how he just wanted to live a normal life. Suddenly they crashed into the car ahead. "This is *not* normal!" the head of house commented.[13]

Henri came to a crash landing in more ways than one at l'Arche Daybreak. However, once he decided to stop running around giving talks and lectures and instead stay put and live more simply, he began to see the fruits of living out what he had recommended to others. The result was a happier, healthier, less conflicted Henri Nouwen, although he would struggle to the very end to keep his life simple and not get caught up in too many projects.

At l'Arche he found a home, and he found that the more he set aside his desires, especially his restless search for new people and experiences to fill his heart, the more the simple vulnerability of the core members and the love of the l'Arche community penetrated him and transformed him. The mutuality and interdependence that are central to l'Arche operate much like these qualities do in a family. In a family, the weak members count just as much as the strong, and the bond of love is the common medium. It is the same at l'Arche.

Henri learned that the secret at the center of the downward, descending way was to identify with Jesus. I think, in fact, that he was not so much interested in simplicity or poverty for their own sake, but as part of the mystery of Christ. For Nouwen, the gospel was becoming not just a message explaining how God long ago brought into being a new spiritual reality through Jesus; he was also coming to see it as a blueprint for how we might live our lives and find God today. Downward mobility was becoming a new way for him to enter into the gospel story.

In truth, this was the living out of a meditation that had begun years earlier. At that earlier time he started to realize, and then to teach, that the Eucharist could be a model of the believer's unity with Christ. In the Eucharist we see the host, the sacred bread, being taken...then blessed...then broken...and then given out. All of these eucharistic actions are mirrored in the life of Jesus. The Lord is *taken* when he is called by God; likewise he is *blessed* in his baptism, *broken* on the Cross, and *given* to the world.

Henri leads us to then consider how this mystery connects with our own lives, and we see the same pattern played out once more in us: we also are *taken*, in that God chooses us, too;

blessed, in that God recognizes and loves us; and *broken*, in that we all suffer from woundedness and misfortune. We are also *given*, because our lives too are offered to the world. This is a profound and beautiful teaching, one that takes us to the heart of the Eucharist, of the gospel, and of Nouwen's message to the Christian world.[14] The point I want to emphasize about this meditation is that it makes a direct connection between the life of Jesus and our lives. Just as following the descending way was a new way of identifying with Christ, so, too, was Nouwen's teaching that our lives and the life of Christ are mirrored in the central rituals of the Eucharist.

Breakthrough

I am happy to say that Henri Nouwen's pursuit of this important insight did not end with his living out the descending way at l'Arche. He continued to meditate on the parallelism between the life of Jesus and his own. This thought helped him to keep Christ at the center, and it helped make the gospels a part of everything that was happening around him. Years passed, and then there came a moment when his meditation, like a plant waiting through winter to blossom and flower, yielded a bigger vision.

   This happened when Henri Nouwen discovered Rembrandt's painting *The Return of the Prodigal Son*. His contemplative study of that painting would eventually lead him to write his most profound and memorable book, also called *The Return of the Prodigal Son*, a book that would have much to say about faith, about fathers and sons, and about God. In his study of this beautiful painting, Henri's meditative approach to theology and his own particular kind of artistic and spiritual seeing are exemplified most clearly. As he peered for hours at Rembrandt's painting, then as he wrote and talked to his friends about what he was seeing, the realization that had begun to form itself long ago as part of his eucharistic meditation came again to the fore. Just as Jesus was the bread taken, blessed, broken, and given, so too he is the prodigal, and so then we are prodigal Christs ourselves. The essential point is that our life in Christ is affected by the life that Jesus lived. If we are also taken, blessed, broken, and given, just as Jesus was, then the gospel story can be our story too.

As we turn now to listen for a moment to his thinking, let us imagine that Henri is not so much building an argument as painting a picture. In his vision, the images and their realities overlap and interpenetrate each other on a broad and colorful canvas:

> I am touching here the mystery that Jesus himself became the prodigal son for our sake. He left the house of his heavenly Father, came to a foreign country, gave away all that he had, and returned through his cross to his Father's home. All of this he did, not as a rebellious son, but as the obedient son, sent out to bring home all the lost children of God. Jesus, who told the story to those who criticized him for associating with sinners, himself lived the long and painful journey that he describes.
>
> When I began to reflect on the parable and Rembrandt's portrayal of it, I never thought of the exhausted young man with the face of a newborn baby as Jesus. But now, after so many hours of intimate contemplation, I feel blessed by this vision. Isn't the broken young man kneeling before his father the "lamb of God that takes away the sin of the world"? Isn't he the innocent one who became sin for us? Isn't he the one who didn't "cling to his equality with God," but "became as human beings are"? Isn't he the sinless Son of

God who cried out on the cross: "My God, my God, why have you forsaken me?" Jesus is the prodigal son of the prodigal Father who gave away everything the Father had entrusted to him so that I could become like him and return with him to his Father's home.

Seeing Jesus himself as the prodigal son goes far beyond the traditional interpretation of the parable. Nonetheless, this vision holds a great secret. I am gradually discovering what it means to say that my sonship and the sonship of Jesus are one, that my return and the return of Jesus are one, that my home and the home of Jesus are one. There is no journey to God outside of the journey that Jesus made. The one who told the story of the prodigal son is the Word of God, "through whom all things came into being." He "became flesh, lived among us," and made us part of his fullness.[15]

"There is no journey to God outside the journey that Jesus made." "My sonship and the sonship of Jesus are one." These are profound words indeed. Through his artistic, meditative process, Henri is pushing the boundaries of the gospel upward and outward, expanding the vision and fashioning new truth from old. As he continued to lose himself in the possibilities flowing from the painting and the gospel, Henri would eventually add to the imagery he was creating something of his own deep feelings of shame and rejection. Clearly, Rembrandt's painting was also saying something about sons and fathers, a theme that had always nagged at Henri's heart. The father in the painting could be seen to be blessing his son, just as Henri had longed to feel truly blessed by his father.

Furthermore, just as the bread is taken and blessed in the Eucharist, now he sees that the blessing of the bread, interwoven with the blessing of Jesus, are all vividly reflected in Rembrandt's painting. In Christ, all are blessed. To receive the

Father's blessing is to be restored, profoundly comforted, and empowered to face all temptations and terrors. As the prodigal was welcomed and embraced, as Christ was blessed, so all the shamed and rejected of this earth may come to know that they are welcomed and blessed, and find in that blessing a consolation that relieves all pain and fear. The bread is blessed as it is lifted up, and Jesus is likewise blessed at his baptism, when God the Father speaks from heaven, calling him "son" and saying he is "well pleased" with him. And that blessing can be ours, too. A blessing stands at the heart of God's presence among us. To be loved, to be *beloved*, is to be recognized and blessed.

Claiming God's Blessing

Thus, the blessing of Christ in the gospel is critically important. Jesus is about to begin his ministry, and before he embarks on that long and fated journey, God speaks to him in front of everyone and says: "You are my Son. I love you and take delight in you. Now go." This fatherly blessing is the cornerstone of Christ's self-knowledge and his certainty. It is his comfort in the face of confusion and suffering. The blessing keeps Jesus strong and enables him to face the temptations of Satan in the desert and all the tribulations that will follow. Even in the life of Christ there was always a struggle. However, the difference is this: Jesus did not allow his own doubts and fears and the world's rejection of him to triumph over the voice that blessed him. He had God's blessing, and he let God's voice echo through his being. We must do the same; we must center ourselves on that voice and that knowledge:

> Home is the center of my being where I can hear the voice that says: "You are my Beloved, on you my favor rests"—the same voice that gave life to the first Adam

and spoke to Jesus, the second Adam; the same voice that speaks to all the children of God and sets them free to live in the midst of a dark world while remaining in the light. I have heard that voice. It has spoken to me in the past and continues to speak to me now. It is the never-interrupted voice of love speaking from eternity and giving life and love whenever it is heard. When I hear that voice, I know that I am home with God and have nothing to fear. As the Beloved of my heavenly Father, "I can walk in the valley of darkness: no evil would I fear"...Jesus has made it clear to me that the same voice that he heard at the River Jordan and on Mount Tabor can also be heard by me. He has made it clear to me that just as he has his home with the Father, so do I. Praying to his Father for his disciples, he says: "They do not belong to the world, any more than I belong to the world. Consecrate them [set them aside] in the truth. As you sent me into the world, I have sent them into the world, and for their sake I consecrate myself so that they too may be consecrated in truth." These words reveal my true dwelling place, my true abode, my true home. Faith is the radical trust that home has always been there and always will be there. The somewhat stiff hands of the father rest on the prodigal's shoulders with the everlasting divine blessing: "You are my Beloved, on you my favor rests."[16]

Slowly, hesitantly, Henri began to probe and test this insight further. Why don't more people grasp such an essential truth? No one thinks of himself or herself as beloved as Jesus was beloved. We do not identify with his blessing or with his life. Most of us cannot imagine that our life and the life of Jesus have any real connection. We cannot imagine this because we know ourselves to be pitiable, full of uncertainty, guilt, and shame. Yet we are called to overcome these negative feelings, as Christ overcame his temptations.

After Christ was blessed, he was tempted. He was tempted by fame, he was tempted to imagine himself to be indestructible, and he was tempted by self-aggrandizement. Henri knew deep down that this list was far from complete. In his own life he had known a certain amount of fame, and he realized that the greatest temptation is not the desire for fame or fortune. The greatest temptation is self-rejection. The biggest spiritual problem is coming to believe that you are worth anything in God's eyes. The negative voices that we so often hear, voices telling us we are of little worth, are deafening. But this is really not God speaking; this is the world's message. Perhaps we tend to believe this message because our life is often so frustrating. We feel that we are not in control and that we are alone. For this reason we are more ready to accept what the world tells us: "You are no-body. You are not loved. Not you." That is how we know that we can never be God's beloved. That is how we know that God may have blessed Jesus, or the saints, or even Henri Nouwen, but not us. We cannot imagine that we also might be God's beloved.

Yet the blessing is ours if we claim it. God's blessing is always available. "You whoever you are are my beloved." These words can undo a life of sorrow and rejection. This is the certainty that Jesus clung to during his temptation and his rejection and his death. "You are my beloved." Indeed, Jesus overcame all opposition and every temptation; such is the power of God's blessing. There is, in fact, probably no greater power than this. We ourselves are drawn into unity with God by God's blessing of Jesus. We are drawn into the life of Jesus through the Spirit, leading us to the Father.

This is all very hard to accept. I myself have heard this message now for many years and I still struggle every day to believe it. Yet I continue to let the message fall on my heart like water on a rock, knowing that the rock will one day yield.

Like the bread we receive, like Jesus himself, we are all taken, blessed, broken, and given. We are all chosen by God, we all receive God's blessing on our lives, we are all wounded and broken by many negative experiences, and we are all given to the world, sent into the world to say yes to God's love.

This implies a much greater connection between Christ and the world. But is what Henri is saying so very new? Yes and no. There have always been voices in Christianity calling for believers to identify with Christ. Paul tells his followers to imitate him, because he is imitating the Lord.[17] He also says that in baptism we "put on" Christ.[18] In the Epistle to the Romans, Christ is called the "first-born of many brothers and sisters."[19] The First Epistle of John says that God has lavished love on us, in that we are his children.[20] However, despite these biblical assurances, Christians have never been entirely comfortable with the idea that they are sharing in the existence of Christ in any personal or real way.

Christ the Son of God is too exalted, too far above us for anyone to truly identify with him. The most that traditional Catholicism would accept was the proposition that we should take Christ as a model of humility and obedience, as Thomas à Kempis proposed in his *Imitation of Christ*. Within the community, the priests alone were considered worthy enough to stand in the place of the Lord. Now Henri is proposing that we open our hearts and try to imagine that all of us can stand in that place. The difference is this: instead of beginning with an unreachable moral ideal, he wants us to first ask ourselves if we can believe that God loves us, that we are God's beloved. Henri Nouwen, the wounded, restless, and shamed prophet of modern Christianity, tells us this is indeed true—that we are not only loved by God, but *beloved* as Christ was beloved, as cherished sons and daughters of the Father.

It is an enormous realization. It is a teaching that, if accepted, has the power to change a person's life dramatically. It is not based on some inscrutable mysticism nor is it a theological abstraction. It means joining, or even merging, my life with the life of Jesus and saying, we are one family at one table, we are connected, and the direction that Jesus is moving is my way, too. Henri had accepted this truth for himself, and he saw that it must apply to all believers in Christ.

Still, in 1992, the same year in which Henri published *The Return of the Prodigal Son*, he was already moving on, extending the vision, and offering this message even to people who felt they had no connection to Jesus. So it was that he wrote another book, *Life of the Beloved*, in which he proposes this spirituality to Fred Bratman, his secular Jewish friend from New York. In that book he tells Fred about sharing in the key moments of the Eucharist, being taken, blessed, broken, and given, and especially about the blessing that Jesus received:

> "You are my Son, the Beloved; my favor rests on you."
> For many years I have read these words and even reflected on them in sermons and lectures, but it is only since our talks in New York that they have taken on a meaning far beyond the boundaries of my own tradition. Our many conversations led me to the inner conviction that the words, "You are my Beloved" revealed the most intimate truth about all human beings, whether they belonged to any particular tradition or not. Fred, all I want to say to you is "You are the Beloved," and all I hope is that you can hear these words as spoken to you with all the tenderness and force that love can hold. My only desire is to make these words reverberate in every corner of your being—"You are the Beloved."[21]

Henri loved Fred and all the people around him, and he knew that God's love was that much greater, much more faithful, and forgiving than his own. Henri's spirituality was in fact molded around his experience of the ever-expanding love of God, a love so great as to encompass every person, and every stage of belief and awareness. Henri's woundedness might have led him to wonder about his own belovedness, but not that of others. So, once Henri became convinced in his own heart that he could claim this blessing from the Father for himself, despite his faults and failings, he wanted everyone to be included. It was as if he had climbed a high mountain peak, and once at the top, found himself on a ridge that led easily to yet another mountaintop in a chain of summits. Gazing down, he was ready to paint a new epic canvas of God's reconciliation of all things—and all people—in Christ.[22] No one was excluded, not the high or the low, not the most secular, the most cynical, or those most deeply wounded. Every prodigal was called forward to receive God's blessing.

This bold and beautiful line of thinking taps a little-explored vein of early Christian experience. Henri began to find other interesting verses in the Bible suggesting that there is more to be said about "putting on Christ" than the initial acceptance of God's blessing. Long ago Henri had learned from Anton Boisen that weakness could become one's strength and inspiration. Now he could see that weakness and humility were essential aspects of the life of Jesus. Christ was born in utter vulnerability and died in weakness. The descending Christ was ultimately a weak and utterly human Christ, someone like us. We all know that Christ shared our condition so that we might share his, but no one had really thought of Christ's descending way as a pathway leading right to our own door.

Maybe the life of Christ was not so different from our own lives, and we are wrong to imagine a huge divide separating us from Christ and the way he lived and died. This new line of thinking is reflected in two books Nouwen wrote during his final, sabbatical year. The first of these, *Bread for the Journey*, is a daybook that includes reflections and admonitions with headings such as "Being Like Jesus," "Claiming the Identity of Jesus" and "Being Clothed in Christ." Henri explains that Jesus and the Father breathe the same Holy Spirit, and that that same Spirit is given to us as well. This same Holy Spirit leads us to total transformation and the realization that Christ is living in us. "Thus," he says, "we are the living Christ in the world. Jesus, who is God-made-flesh, continues to reveal himself in our own flesh. Indeed, *true salvation is becoming Christ*"[23] (italics added).

"We are the living Christ in the world." Henri said this not about ministers or priests or missionaries or nuns or monks, but about ordinary people, even those who could not claim any special accomplishments, good deeds, or even possession of a great deal of faith. Christ reaches everyone, and his life and death are universal events:

> Jesus' death is a death for all humanity, and Jesus' resurrection is a resurrection for all humanity. Not one person from the past, present, or future is excluded from the great passage of Jesus from slavery to freedom, from the land of captivity to the promised land, from death to eternal life.[24]

Adam, God's Beloved

In the second book written during his final sabbatical, *Adam: God's Beloved*, Henri moves his new theory about Christ from the abstract to the concrete. As he had done with his book for Fred Bratman, he began this book by following his own heart, and wrote out of his own strong feelings of love and attachment. Actually, he was originally planning to write something about the Apostle's Creed during his sabbatical, but while he was researching that topic, he received news that Adam, his l'Arche friend, was dying. He rushed from Boston to Toronto and was able to be with Adam and his family when Adam died. Adam had been a very special person in Henri's life, and as he looked at him lying in his coffin, and realized that Adam was thirty-four, the same age Christ had been at death, he suddenly understood that he needed to write, not about the Apostle's Creed, but about Adam. So it was that in this last book, about Adam Arnett, Nouwen brought his long meditation on the descending way and being beloved and sharing in the life of Christ to a magnificent conclusion.[25]

Who was Adam Arnett? Adam was a core member of l'Arche, and the most disabled person living at Daybreak. At the beginning of Henri's sojourn there, he had been assigned to do a morning routine with Adam, who was almost completely immobile, unable to speak and unable to make eye contact. Confronted by the physical needs of someone who could not speak or even move in any coordinated way, Henri was initially confused. Frankly, he saw little point in spending valuable time tending Adam. He was also frightened at being so completely out of his element. He was lucky if he could move his own body through space without incident—what if he accidentally hurt Adam? It took a lot of encouragement from others to convince Henri that he was up to the task of caring for Adam for a few hours every day. Then, like a child taking his first wobbly attempts at riding a bicycle, Henri was delighted to realize that he was able to do these very physical tasks he had been asked to do.

He also realized something else. Adam was not the mute and inscrutable burden he had first appeared to be. Adam was aware of who was with him, and Adam somehow made those around him feel more at peace. Henri began to talk to Adam, telling Adam what he was doing and what he was thinking, and began to feel very assured and comforted in the intimacy that grew up between them. The many hours that Henri Nouwen spent caring for Adam and talking to Adam became, in the end, a religious experience and another kind of contemplation.

Just as Henri had, after many hours, come to discern the face of Jesus in the figure of the prodigal son in Rembrandt's painting, so he also found Christ in the figure of Adam. This slow realization began with Henri's growing sense that Adam's life had a purpose and a mission. A number of people were deeply affected by their encounters with Adam. He brought peace, even healing, to those around him. In his own way he was doing God's work, just as Jesus had. What was more, Henri was coming to see that Jesus' life had contained many hidden periods and many ordinary experiences, too. There were times when both Jesus and Adam had been equally vulnerable. Jesus had lived a whole human life, beginning with the utter vulnerability of infancy. By embracing the weakness and limitations of ordinary life and existence, the incarnate Christ had made all of life holy. Henri's meditative time spent with Adam was making this all the more clear. In his unique way, Adam was living the life of Jesus:

Jesus did not come in power and might. He came dressed in weakness. The greatest part of his life was hidden, sharing the human condition of a baby, a young child, a struggling adolescent, and a maturing adult. Adam's hidden life, like the life of Jesus of Nazareth, was an unseen preparation for the time of his ministry to many people, even though neither he nor his parents looked on it that way.

I am not saying that Adam was a second Jesus. But I am saying that because of the vulnerability of Jesus we can see Adam's extremely vulnerable life as a life of utmost spiritual significance. Adam did not have unique heroic virtues: he did not excel at anything that newspapers write about. But I am convinced that Adam was chosen to witness to God's love through his brokenness. To say this is not to romanticize him or to be sentimen-

tal. Adam was, like all of us, a limited person, more limited than most, and unable to express himself in words.
But he was also a whole person and a blessed man. In
his weakness he became a unique instrument of God's
grace. He became a revelation of Christ among us.[26]

The mute, wordless nature of Adam's witness to Christ
would not have been completely foreign to Henri Nouwen. Although his own life and ministry revolved around words and
verbal communication, he had spent many years studying, and
even participating in, a type of monasticism that sees silence as
a spiritual form of being and a form of prayer. His sojourn in
the Cistercian Abbey of the Genesee followed years of interest
in monasticism and teaching and writing about the desert fathers. The desert fathers were the first Christian monks. These
early monks went into the desert seeking isolation in an attempt to reach a level of encounter with God that would go beyond images and beyond words. They were the first Christians
to practice silence, albeit in informal ways, as the following
desert-father story illustrates. The speaker is relating a story
from when he was a young, would-be monk, looking for a
teacher:

> Abba Isaac said, "When I was younger, I lived with
> Abba Chronios. He would never tell me to do any work,
> although he was old and tremulous; but he himself got
> up and offered food to me and to everyone. Then I lived
> with Abba Theodore of Pherme and he did not tell me
> to do anything either, but he himself set the table and
> said to me, 'Brother, if you want to, come and eat.' I
> replied, 'I have come to you to help you, why do you
> never tell me to do anything?' But the old man gave me
> no reply whatever. So I went to tell the old men. They

came and said to him, 'Abba, the brother has come to
your holiness in order to help you. Why do you never
tell him to do anything?' The old man said to them,
'Am I a cenobite,[27] that I should give him orders? As far
as I am concerned, I do not tell him anything, but if he
wishes he can do what he sees me doing.' From that
moment I took the initiative and did what the old man
was about to do. As for him, what he did, he did in silence; so he taught me to work in silence."[28]

From his immersion in such stories, Henri was well aware
that God is manifest in silence, and he once wrote a little book
on this spirituality called *The Way of the Heart.*[29] Henri found a
way to evoke the spirit of silent monasteries when writing
Adam: God's Beloved by including among the people who
learned important lessons from Adam a monk, in fact an abbot
whom I knew and who had inspired me when I made regular
visits to his monastery in the late seventies.

Fr. Bruno, the abbot of the Camoldolese hermitage in Big
Sur, California, had, after eighteen years of service as an abbot,
gone to stay with Henri for three months at Daybreak. His
time as an abbot was over, and he wanted to spend more time
with the disabled. At Daybreak he made a natural connection
with Adam. A man of silence himself, he quickly confirmed
what Henri and others had felt: to those with ears to hear and
eyes to see, Adam was a teacher. Adam even taught this experienced abbot, Fr. Bruno, something regarding the monastic life
that Fr. Bruno knew so well. From Adam's example of silence,
Fr. Bruno learned what it means to empty oneself even further
of thoughts, feelings, and passions and enter more completely
the deep solitude of God.[30]

Like Fr. Bruno, Henri also accepted Adam's role as a
teacher in his life. But what Henri saw most clearly in Adam

was the face of Christ. His book about Adam's life is modeled on the traditional idea of the life of Jesus: first, a hidden life, then the desert, then public life, passion, death, and resurrection. By superimposing the life of Christ onto the life of Adam, Nouwen not only gives Adam a dignity that few others would have considered reasonable or proper, he makes his final and boldest statement about the purpose of the Incarnation and of the lives we all live today:

> I recognized many parallels between the story of Jesus and the story of Adam. And I knew something else. I knew, in a very profound place, that Adam, in some mysterious way, had become an image of the living Christ for me just as Jesus, when he lived on the earth, was friend, teacher, and guide for his disciples. In and through Adam I came to a truly new understanding of those relationships of Jesus, not just as they were lived long ago, but as Jesus desires to live them now, with me and with us, through the weakest and most vulnerable people. Indeed, not only did I come to know more about God by caring for Adam, but also Adam helped me, by his life, to discover and rediscover the Spirit of Jesus alive in my own "poorness of spirit." Jesus lived long ago, but Adam lived in my time. Jesus was physically present to his disciples. Adam was physically present to me. Jesus was Emmanuel, God with us. Adam became for me a sacred person, a holy man, an image of the living God.
>
> Was Adam very unusual? Was he some special angel? Not at all. Adam was one person among many others. But I had a relationship with Adam, and he became special for me. I loved him, and our relationship was one of the most significant of my life.[31]

Here then, is what Henri learned from Adam and what he taught about the descending way, about our being God's Beloved, and about putting on Christ: God is love; the descending way is the way of love, and the Incarnation is far from over. Wherever love blossoms and relationships form, wherever we show vulnerability or we foster intimacy with another person, there we find Christ and we find God. Perhaps Henri did not need Adam to learn this lesson; he could have read it in the Bible, or even in Victor Hugo, but Adam served as a reminder that there are different ways of learning something. By bathing and caring for Adam, by holding him in his arms and feeding him, Henri experienced some of the physical intimacy he had craved all his life. He did something essential and physical that involved the body of another person. This is very different from merely talking about intimacy, or even having an intimate conversation. Adam himself was a special person, marginalized in ways few of us can comprehend. Adam embodied for Henri a humanity that suffered, yet bore a great light and a great promise. In Adam Henri could see the face of the poor, descending Christ, and he could see his own face reflected as well. In Adam Henri found not only a teacher but also a brother, someone who seemed to yearn silently for all that Henri yearned for and, like Henri himself, brought many to peace despite his handicaps and his weakness.

Discerning the Spirit

I have traced a line through Henri's teaching and through his experiences and thoughts about Jesus, beginning with his eucharistic meditation and ending with his loving alignment of the life of Adam with the life of Christ. I always felt that Henri was working out his thoughts about Jesus in a purposeful manner, but I am much more aware of the connections now than before. A bigger picture is emerging for me. In the last years of his life, Henri was developing an insight that can be found in Paul's writings and in the gospels, but that had never been adequately addressed by the great teachers of Christian history. Yet it is something we all know intuitively to be true. Mother Teresa said that she worked among the dying and the poorest of the poor in Calcutta because she saw in them the face of Christ. We have accepted the truth of her statement, but we have failed to realize that when we look in our mirrors, we must see Christ's face there, also. In the descending way, Jesus comes to all of us.

We meet Christ in the poor and the dying, but we also meet him in every small sorrow and triumph and concern of our own lives. This was Henri's teaching. Without a hint of fundamentalism, Henri Nouwen sensed Christ's presence everywhere around him. His meditations, his ministry, his life with friends and community—everything was part of a larger reality, part of the kingdom of God. What he saw, he spoke and wrote down and taught to others, with the result that we see that vision, too.

All visions of Christ blossom and fade; they fall to the earth and die. Later they spring up again where we least expect them. Jesus himself used the analogy of a mustard seed or a sudden breath of wind. It takes real wisdom to discern the true presence of Jesus. In the desert-father story above, we see the young novice searching for an abba, so that he can be a disciple and begin to truly learn. In all such stories the teacher is very important.

Perhaps in this chapter we see the same thing: to be disciples we also need a teacher, and Abba Henri's bold exploration of the promise of Christ's kingdom is a teaching for us all, a teaching that places all God's children under the Father's mantle and calls each one "My Beloved."

6
SPIRITUALITY AND PRAYER

Living the Life

In this last chapter I want to say something about Henri Nouwen's own spiritual experience. Henri had a particular way of being a spiritual person that I could never describe completely, or in detail, but I nevertheless want to talk about briefly as a way to end my "reading" of Henri. None of what I am about to discuss here constitutes a big topic, such as the Eucharist, or Jesus, or the Church. The things I want to address now are more subjective issues that fit best under the rubric of personal spirituality.

The entertainer Danny Kaye once said, "Life is a great big canvas, and you should throw all the paint on it you can." These words are an openhearted, exuberant declaration, and one that might seem to sum up much of what we have seen about Henri's spirituality so far. However, although I have referred to Henri many times as someone with an artistic sensibility, and despite Henri's creative and affirming embrace of life, I doubt that he would have agreed with Danny Kaye's pleasant sentiment. I say this because Henri Nouwen's goal was never to bring color or excitement to the world, nor was he trying to make a statement with his life.

In fact, although he chronicled many of his numerous adventures and experiences in his books, I doubt that he went anywhere, did anything, or made any friendship in order to write about it, or be seen doing something interesting or colorful. He had very different motivations and ideas about life's purpose. Instead of seeing life as an opportunity to make a big splash, I think that Henri Nouwen essentially saw life as a gift, and the creation of life as an expression of God's love. It therefore follows that how we live becomes part of our conversation with God, and our words and actions form a response to our having been not only created, but loved. Henri went out and did things in the world because he was living out his experience of God's love.

However, I cannot say that Henri was on some sort of divine mission. He did not plan to have a great impact on so many; it just happened. The world that Henri saw around him was full of people. Their humanity attracted him, and their need for light and inspiration called out to him, but that was not what made him write so creatively or love so many of them. Instead, Henri Nouwen's considerable contribution to Christian spirituality was based on a decision, renewed again and again, to be true to himself. If life is a response to God's love, then part of our response is to see ourselves, be ourselves, own who we are, and speak from our hearts. Henri's personal spirituality revolved around his realizing and embracing his own identity.

Therefore Henri Nouwen created a spirituality that, in the first place, felt right to him. Henri's ego, his own journey, his personal doubts and concerns were all big parts of his message to the world. It is interesting that, although he took this introspective, almost egocentric position, Henri never appeared to be "navel-gazing," or overly self-absorbed.

Sometimes a handicap becomes a source of strength. Many great achievements begin with overcoming adversity. In Nouwen's case, his deep sense of shame and his difficulty in feeling security and attachment were handicaps that led him to focus on himself to an unusual degree. He needed both to understand himself and to believe in himself in order to find peace, and this was a long and difficult process. He certainly was on a psychological journey, as well as on a spiritual one, but he did not frame his journey in psychological terms. Interestingly, without evoking any formal philosophical language to express what he was doing, he seemed to be living out a kind of existentialism.

Existentialism was one of the dominant currents in art and ideas during Henri's formative years. It focuses on the importance of self-awareness and recognition of the human predicament. A parallel between Henri and Kierkegaard has already been noted,[1] and Kierkegaard was an existentialist. Rather than being self-absorbed, Henri Nouwen was self-aware in an existential sense, and that is an important difference.

One of the reasons why I can say that Henri was not self-absorbed is that he was never small-minded or provincial. He could talk about personal things without becoming petty or narrow. He spent very little time in the end thinking of himself as a priest, or a Roman Catholic, or a Dutchman, or even a European. All those qualifiers he regarded more as accidental aspects of his life, rather than part of his essence. He was Henri Nouwen, and that meant being a special, unique individual, but an individual like other people everywhere.

Personality and Spiritual Practice

As I said earlier, Henri created a spirituality tailored to his own measure. It may be useful here to recall momentarily what we learned in chapter 2 with regard to Nouwen's psychology. I think the most helpful psychological concept or model we considered there was the Myers Briggs Personality Inventory. We saw that Henri fit the ENFP type rather closely, and that many of his somewhat unusual quirks seem more comprehensible once we realize that Henri was a classic ENFP. As we consider his personal spirituality, let us return to that ENFP model and the Myers Briggs perspective.

The Myers Briggs test can form an important component in spiritual direction, because many people enter this type of counseling feeling that a one-size-fits-all approach to prayer and spirituality no longer satisfies them. Spiritual directors often know quite a bit about the MBTI.[2] One spiritual director, Msgr. Chester Michael, has even created a complete program of spiritual exercises based on the Myers Briggs classifications. These are presented in a book entitled *Prayer and Temperament*. Among many other things, *Prayer and Temperament* explores the "NF" (Intuition and Feeling) personality and spiritual experience. Because Nouwen was ENFP, he would have been part of this NF family. Here is how Msgr. Michael and his co-author, Marie Norrisey, describe the general type:

> NF persons are usually creative, optimistic, verbal, persuasive, outspoken, good at both writing and speaking. They have a great need for self-expression and communicate with others easily. NFs are good listeners, good at counselling, good at resolving conflicts and making peace. They hate conflict and are unable to operate at peak efficiency when the situation becomes tense and strained. They like to have face-to-face encounters and are able to read faces and catch non-verbal communications. NFs have deep feelings and are upset if treated impersonally. They find it difficult to handle negative criticism, and become discouraged when meeting a negative attitude in others, but blossom under affirmation. They freely give and need strokes and communicate their own enthusiasm

to others. They need acceptance, support, and prefer cooperation rather than competition.

NFs are highly committed to helping others and usually relate well to those who befriend them. They are enthusiastic, insightful, full of empathy, understanding, and compassion. They see in others possibilities for good that other temperaments do not perceive. Being person-oriented they are apt to have favorites, but persons are always more important than things. Because Thinking and Sensing are their Interior Functions, NFs must make a special effort to be logical and correct in their thinking and to be aware of details and routine.

NFs are always searching for meaning, authenticity, self-identity. They have a great urge for perfection and wholeness and are quite idealistic. They have a hunger for integrity and are willing to make great sacrifices to attain it. Personal growth and development are necessities for both themselves and anyone for whom they feel a responsibility. They are the natural rescuers of those in trouble, and this leads to the danger of becoming too involved in others' problems...

Self-improvement, self-development, self-actualization are at the top of the list of their priorities. NFs have a tremendous hunger and thirst for growth in their inner life; and for those who believe in God, this can be satisfied only in prayer, spiritual reading, contemplation. They experience a great need for periods of quiet and silence in order to make contact with their inner selves. "How can I become the person that I am supposed to be?" "How can I become truly real, authentic, and true to my own unique self?", are questions uppermost in the mind of the NF.[3]

Well, that certainly sounds like Henri Nouwen! In fact, as one reads this passage, it is important to keep in mind that the person being described is the "typical NF," not Henri Nouwen himself. I have quoted at length from this profile because it reaffirms that much of Henri's remarkable persona simply sprang from his temperament. His hunger for God, his urge to write, his unbounded concern for others, his idealism, and the intensity of his friendships and presence are all reflected in this description. The close correlation between the model and Henri's predilections means that Henri became such a faithful and inspiring witness to Christianity not by altering his personality to fit the norms of his faith, nor by being all things to all people, but simply by being his true, "NF" self.

Chester Michael calls the NF the "Augustinian type," because he sees St. Augustine as an exemplar of this sort of person. If this is true, then it is somewhat ironic that, by being himself, Henri may have ended up acting very much like a long line of similarly-innovative Christian figures going back at least to St. Augustine. Henri certainly was not trying to copy or be like any earlier saint or mystic, and Augustine was in many ways very different from Henri, but they still had some things in common.

I did ask Henri once if he felt any affinity for Augustine, and he admitted that he also was a "confessional" writer, putting his writings in a category that Augustine created. I am sure Henri thought of Augustine as too stern and intellectual for him, but Augustine was also very personal and creative. St. Augustine was the first person in history to write a book about his real feelings, instead of what one "ought" to feel.[4] In its day, Augustine's *Confessions* broke all the rules.[5] He abandoned stereotypes and bared his heart with all its faults. Henri also broke rules in a similar way, as we have seen in the last few chapters.

The Augustinian type is obviously very self-aware and prefers to deal creatively with spiritual images and issues. Msgr.

Michael presents a program tailored to this personality type, just as he does for each group he identifies.[6] For the NF person he suggests the following spiritual exercise: they are to pick a selection of verses from the Bible and ask how these verses can be made personally relevant today. This is a process that uses a type of creative imagination he calls "transposition."[7] As we saw in the third chapter concerning Henri's artistic approach, an open-ended, creative exposition of biblical imagery was something Henri did naturally, without anyone telling him he would find it appealing. It can hardly be a coincidence that Henri engaged in "transposition" all the time. By immersing himself in contemplation and in expansive, prayerful writing, he was doing exactly what would be most comfortable and profitable for his type. Creativity, imagination, feeling, and intuition are fundamental to how NF persons express their true selves. As Msgr. Michael tells it, this creative process can become intense as the NF seeks to include everyone in the new vision:

> The NF needs to find meaning in everything. The NF wants to know that what one does makes a difference; that each person can make a unique contribution; that he/she is important; that God loves each one of us unconditionally, as we are now, sins and all. The NF needs to be assured of this every day in order to keep growing into a deeper and more intimate relationship with God. Experiencing a personal relationship with God is the one essential element of any authentic NF spirituality. Therefore, daily prayer and quiet are a "must" for persons of this temperament.
>
> The NF derives a heightened sense of meaning from every event and relationship by constantly seeking the hidden meaning of things. Through Intuition

and creative imagination, the NF is able to give new meaning to life's experiences, a meaning beyond the mere external event of the here and now.[8]

Again, this description draws an uncannily precise portrait of Henri Nouwen's spiritual experience. One could substitute the word "Henri" for the words "the NF" in this passage with nearly complete accuracy. In fact, one could move directly from these remarks by Michael and Norrisey to *The Inner Voice of Love*, *Adam: God's Beloved*, *The Genesee Diary*, or any of the more personal Nouwen books to find these observations exemplified.

What these passages from Michael and Norrisey's *Prayer and Temperament* help me to see is that Henri was not living out, nor was he presenting to the world, a universally applicable spiritual program, perhaps because there is no "universally applicable" spiritual program. He began with what he sensed was true of himself and could feel in his own person. He was very confident that his heartfelt individual faith, even in its Roman Catholic specificity, had a ring of truth to it that would have universal appeal. He was right. Just as in the case of St. Augustine before him, Henri's simple books about his true feelings had, and continue to have, an enormous impact on Christians everywhere. The immense appeal of Nouwen's books and his message reminds us that it is not necessary to have an NF personality or be Roman Catholic in order to be moved and affected by Nouwen's message of faith and love.

Henri's close correlation with the ENFP model was an indicator of his own authenticity. In fact, it was easy for him to live the Nouwen spirituality because he was NF and he *was* Henri Nouwen. This is an essential point. In fact, for me, understanding this reinforces a spiritual insight I learned from another great teacher I was privileged to know well, and someone I also introduced to Henri, an Englishman named Donald Nicholl.

Donald Nicholl was a professor of history and a Catholic thinker who put his remarkable intellect and spiritual gifts to good use in explaining the world to others. He died in 1997, shortly after Henri himself died. Besides writing and teaching, Nicholl was sought after by individuals, groups, and communities for spiritual guidance, and he was also active in peace work, particularly in Israel.[9] While staying with him at his house in the English Midlands, I asked Donald one day about holiness, a topic about which he had written an important book.[10] He said this:

> One thing that is clear is that it should not be hard to be holy. If you spend time around Mother Teresa you realize that she is not making any great effort to be who she is. Now, compare her to Tolstoy, who spent his life making lists of resolutions, and then new lists, and then tearing them all up in frustration—for Mother Teresa, it's not like that. It's all very natural.

The same can be said of Henri. Despite his persistent restlessness and periodic agonizing over his life, Henri was very natural, very true to who he really was, and that is one reason why he brought so much light into the world, and why his message was so believable and engaging. I cannot say he was entirely comfortable with who he was, but he knew who he was and did not try to be someone else. Henri's authenticity was really part of his personal sincerity. We have already seen how much Nouwen's incredible openness and sincere engagement impressed his readers and the people he met. Henri was deeply and truly interested in his friends and those around him, as the earlier remarks by Fred Rogers illustrate so well.[11] People were simply amazed at how much Henri Nouwen seemed to care about them personally, whoever they were.

Sincerity of Heart

Henri's sincerity was a factor in far more than his friendships. It was a fundamental aspect of his spirituality, too. Henri was honest about his doubts, but equally honest about his certainty. He was a sincere Christian believer who spoke out of his own profound sense of God's reality. Because he was so certain of the truth of Christianity, and because he brought his personal, existentialist, and confessional twist to questions of belief, many persons who harbored deep doubts or had little faith came to believe in the gospel because of him. His faith and conviction were contagious because his sincerity was not feigned or part of a program.

This is an important point. There are those who consciously make a spiritual sacrifice to "believe what is unbelievable." They submit to the authority of the Church or believe the truth of the Bible "on faith," and thus attempt to override any doubts that may remain in their minds. This is not wrong, or somehow a bad idea, but it was not Henri Nouwen's way. Instead of deciding to accept everything on faith, Nouwen's sincere embrace of the gospel stemmed, I believe, from a paring, or narrowing-down, of a great deal of dogma and a refocusing on what was essential to Christian belief. I once made a passing comment to Henri about orthodoxy, and he interrupted what I was saying to remark, "If you believe in the Creeds, you are orthodox. Period." He had strong feelings on this point. As he saw it, many of the people who were arguing about whether their beliefs or someone else's were correct should simply accept each other. He pared orthodoxy down to a minimum. Although Henri was a very faithful priest, he was not invested in the defense or the promotion of the entire history or agenda or doctrinal structure of Roman Catholicism. He once told me he thought this was a waste of energy.

Instead, we see Henri assuming a very Vatican II posture, putting Jesus at the center and openly evaluating traditional doctrines and practices for their usefulness to the modern believer. Not everything applies, but some things do. A faith that is real must be both creative and conscious of the form that faith has taken in earlier generations. Freedom and commitment are equally important. We see his approach illustrated in a piece he wrote when he was asked to give a talk on Mary. On that occasion he began with the words:

Speaking about Mary, the mother of God and now our mother, requires great honesty as well as simplicity. In all honesty, I want to tell you that only recently has Mary come close to me. During this past Holy Week while staying with the Trappists in Holland, Manitoba, I knew that I was being asked to live the death and rising of Jesus in my own flesh, but I also knew that I couldn't do it alone. It would destroy me.

On the day before I left to go to the Trappists, a friend had given me a rosary of the seven sorrows of Mary. Frankly speaking, I didn't even know which the seven sorrows were! But as I learned about them, I realized that this rosary had been given to me so that Mary could show me how to be truly faithful to her Son. "Stabat Mater," Mary stood by me as I asked Jesus to let me die with him and rise with him. She stood by me as I tried to let go of the many people and things that so far had prevented me from being nothing but a child of God. She stood by me as I tried to strip myself of all the busyness, craziness and activism that had made me into a "respected priest." She stood by me as I begged God to raise me up with Jesus into a new life, maybe hidden from the world but visible to

God. She stood by me when I expressed, against all the
yearnings of my flesh, the desire to know no one but
the crucified and risen Lord and to give all of my being
into his service.[12]

This is what I see happening in this passage: As Henri begins his talk on Mary we see him confronting a nucleus of traditional Catholic spiritual images—the Rosary, the Seven
Sorrows, the *Stabat Mater.* He admits that none of this is very
familiar to him, but apparently he was able to learn that behind
the feast of Our Lady of Sorrows (September 15) there had
been several older feast days in Catholicism that were meditations on "seven sorrows" that Mary suffered. In the fourteenth
century a poem was written for these medieval feast-day litur-
gies. This poem was widely known as *Stabat Mater*, which is
Latin for "the mother stood (at the foot of the Cross)." The
Stabat Mater was put to different settings of liturgical music
many times over the centuries.

So how does Henri deal with these Marian devotions? We
see that he begins with a disclaimer. He says that in the past he
has been very little attracted to Mary. He also speaks about a
recent spiritual crisis and about Jesus. Then, without endorsing
the praying of special rosaries or celebrating the ancient feasts
of the Church, he allows the image of Mary and of her con-
stancy to enter his meditations. Just recently she had stood by
him personally, as she stood by Jesus, while he struggled to divest himself of his anxious thoughts and burdens. As a mother,
she has helped him realize he is a child of God. Henri admits
that Mary has not been a normal part of his devotions, but he
shows us how he is learning to regard her. In a very short para-
graph, Henri dives to the heart of what Mary can mean to him
and to us. He uses the traditional devotions as a springboard to
enter his own meditation, which concerns being a child of
God. Four times he repeats the words, "she stood by me."

This example is typical of the way in which Henri dealt with traditional Christian beliefs and devotions. The result of Nouwen's approach is not to end up with nothing, or to finally pronounce that everything is relative. Without announcing what he was doing, Henri Nouwen represented to those who listened to him a Vatican II return to the essentials of Christian faith—Christ Jesus, the gospel, and Eucharist. These were the center of Christian experience, and Henri's sincere acceptance of an orthodox understanding of these central elements of Christian faith, and of the ethical implications of the gospel, formed one of the core elements of his spirituality. Because he believed in and held to the core of Christian faith, the other practices and beliefs did not alienate him, nor did they distract him.

Belief was, in fact, the unspoken essence of his spirituality. Henri lived the gospel story because he first believed the gospel story. His great faith is all the more remarkable because, in the university environment where he chose to work, basic Christian doctrines are often questioned or dismissed as disproven or outmoded. In this regard, I think that Henri Nouwen surprised just about everyone. When theologians or people in ministry are as open and candid about their true thoughts and feelings as Henri was, we normally expect to hear that they don't really believe everything they are supposed to believe. This was certainly the case in 1963, when John A. T. Robinson, the Anglican bishop, published his *Honest to God*. Henri, by contrast, was perfectly honest in upholding all the basic truths of Christianity, not because they had been handed down by tradition, but because he thought that they were true.

This is certainly one reason why his message held together and was so widely accepted. He was effective because he spoke as a reformer who believed in what he was reforming. Just as Jesus claimed to uphold the law, and revealed the law's true meaning, Henri Nouwen sincerely upheld the central tenets of Christianity, but then looked at the Christian tradition from a new angle to get at its true meaning. His approach was personal and intuitive, rather than intellectual. Nevertheless, it was powerful and persuasive, and it touched people from every sort of background. Henri's candor in admitting his frustrations and weaknesses established his credibility. Then, because he promoted and explained the gospel as something he also knew to be true, and did not merely accept on faith or out of obligation, he became an inspiration to all who needed encouragement in their acceptance of Christian principles.

The Limitations of Mysticism

Although Christian mysticism would normally be a topic of great importance for a teacher of spirituality, Henri Nouwen took little interest in mystics or other classic figures in the history of Christianity. His friend Robert Jonas has told me he thought that Henri didn't have the patience to study someone like John of the Cross or Teresa of Avila. In my own observation, mysticism seemed to put him off, and he seemed a little wary of people who had a mystical bent themselves. There was one exception I know of. While in France, he became interested in a French mystic named Marthe Robin and went to the village where she had lived.[13] Marthe Robin was a stigmatic whose sufferings were linked in some mysterious way to those of Jesus. She lived for decades in visionary solitude, bedridden with pain and subsisting solely on the Eucharist. She was an unimportant person in the world's eyes, and a quite isolated and helpless one, but God was present in her life in a big way. Her mystical experiences had a great impact on French spirituality.

In Marthe Robin we see a real mystic who embodied some of Nouwen's favorite issues: living with Jesus, the paramount importance of the Eucharist, and God working in secret with the unnoticed people of our world. However, Marthe Robin is the exception that proves the rule. In general, Nouwen was not interested in mystical or advanced spiritual states or experiences.

I once saw this illustrated clearly at Harvard. In his lectures on spirituality Henri briefly touched on the traditional doctrine of the Three Ways—the Purgative, the Illuminative, and the Unitive. These stages of spiritual development begin with ascetical self-control and end in mystical cooperation with God. In fact, they are traced ultimately back to Evagrius Ponticus.[14] Henri remarked that in his own seminary days a professor of his had explained the Three Ways with this analogy, "In the first stage, you row the boat, in the second the wind pushes the boat, and in the third, you row *and* the wind pushes the boat." Then Henri laughed and dismissed this traditional model with a wave of his hand. "None of this matters," he said, "because nobody here is even going to reach stage two!"

It was Nouwen's experience that most mystically oriented models of the spiritual life are so far outside the real life experience of ordinary mortals that it does little good to think about them or to study them, just as he had little interest in the lives or the writings of the acknowledged masters of the spiritual life. Studying spirituality by working over such texts might be worthwhile for some people, but for Nouwen, this type of study was too abstract and too intellectual. It lacked immediacy and fostered the belief that spirituality pertained to some higher realm inhabited by spiritual giants or chosen saints of God. Spirituality became something you read about in the library.

What mattered to Henri was not identifying the stages of mystical encounter, but learning to pray in humility and truth. Henri led his university students out of the library and asked them to consider who they really were. That was the beginning of prayer. Prayer is the most subjective and the most personal aspect of the spiritual life. In many ways prayer is the true barometer of one's religion, the place where either there is an authentic connection or there is not. For Henri Nouwen personally, prayer was a place of solace and the revelation of a deeper reality that he drew on throughout his years of ministry.

A Life of Prayer

Because he was a teacher of spirituality, prayer was naturally a topic that Henri needed to address and explain, and he did so frequently. He confidently held prayer up as the solution to suffering, to pain and confusion, and to alienation and distance from God. It is perhaps typical of all pastoral sermons and writings about spirituality to stress the centrality of prayer and offer prayer as the solution to every sort of problem. Yet there was something different in the message of Henri Nouwen, something that was not found in other messages extolling the importance of prayer. Those other messages usually strike me as somewhat predictable and unimaginative—what they seem to be doing is reminding one of a duty, such as wearing a seatbelt or eating a balanced diet. When I hear those messages, I come away feeling like I have been duly reminded and admonished to not be so neglectful and to pursue a disciplined life of prayer and meditation. Nouwen's approach to prayer was different. It may not have been completely original, but it was alive with the vibrancy and authenticity that Nouwen brought to everything.

There was an intensity that was part of many of Henri's personal relationships, and I am sure that that intensity was part of Henri's prayer life too. God was not spared any of Nouwen's insistence or strong feelings. In prayer Henri sought the intimacy and love that he never was able to securely feel among his family and friends. He held onto the knowledge gained in prayer that God loved and accepted him just as he was. I think this was one of the most important dynamics of his prayer life, the knowledge that God knew the secrets of his heart, but God did not reject him.

Out in the world, Henri had to watch himself, because he could be too intense for some people, but when he was alone with God, Nouwen knew he could pour out his heart and would still find acceptance. So, like the woman in the gospel who wore down the unscrupulous judge with her endless clamor,[15] Henri Nouwen engaged in long and intense sessions of prayer that must have yielded results. When there were no results, this was not forgotten by Nouwen. Sometimes later Nouwen would let pass a remark in his writing or speaking that showed that he still felt resentment over something that God had not heard or not done. Like the woman in the gospel, he refused to drop his case. These occasionally intense sessions with God were not always satisfying, because Nouwen was not easily satisfied, but was a restless sort of person, always pressing on. Still, they formed the basis for Nouwen's deep certainties about God, certainties that gave him a foundation upon which he was able to stand in confidence as he reinterpreted so much of Christian spirituality.

For those who would like to read a complete treatment of Nouwen's thoughts and experience of God in prayer, I recommend the compilation by Wendy Greer called *The Only Necessary Thing*.[16] All that I wish to add to that collection and to what I have already said here is that I see an interesting evolution in Nouwen's thought and teaching regarding prayer. That evolution, which took place over many years, reflects his growing maturity and experience and his increasing confidence as a teacher of spirituality.

In his early years Henri was especially concerned with moving prayer from the realm of formal obligation and task fulfillment to that of personal encounter and growth. Much of his thinking about prayer was complemented by and intertwined with his own psychological studies and his association with the pastoral counseling movement. In those years, prayer for Nouwen was part of self-knowledge and psychological growth, and in prayer one discovered new dimensions of expression and being, much as Martin Buber exemplified in his classic *I and Thou*.[17]

Some new elements began to emerge in Nouwen's thinking when he discovered Thomas Merton. Merton opened up for Henri an enticing vista of the world of contemplation and a way of seeing not only God but also the world through new eyes. Merton's new way of seeing was part artistic sensibility, part prayer, and part psychology. If ever there was a time when Henri Nouwen wished to enter the realm of the spiritual masters or dedicate himself to a higher spiritual path, it was when he fell under the spell of Cistercian monasticism and the writings of Thomas Merton.

However, when he did begin to make extended monastic retreats under the direction of Abbot John Eudes Bamberger, the Freudian psychoanalyst-turned-monk who had been trained by Thomas Merton, he realized that the higher path was also a lower path. What he found in the monastery was manual labor, painful solitude, and a fresh encounter with his own myriad personal issues. To his credit, he began to see that all of these things could be a part of the life of prayer, rather than something alien to it. Distractions and mental focus were issues that his director was well-equipped to speak about. Abbot John Eudes was at the time attempting to bring to realization one of Thomas Merton's unfinished projects.

Merton had been the first monk in the United States not only to study Zen but to go beyond Zen and other Eastern contemplative attitudes and philosophies in considering the surprisingly Zen-like spirituality that flourished among the early Christian desert fathers. Among other things, Merton discovered in the desert fathers a search for authenticity that captivated him and must have captivated Henri Nouwen, too. Merton saw the desert fathers as achieving exactly what he and Nouwen were trying so hard to bring about:

What the Fathers sought most of all was their own true self, in Christ. And in order to do this, they had to reject completely the false, formal self, fabricated under social compulsion in "the world." They sought a way to God that was uncharted and freely chosen, not inherited from others who had mapped it out beforehand. They sought a God whom they alone could find, not one who was "given" in a set, stereotyped form by somebody else.[18]

The desert fathers created a community of authentic seekers who advanced in spirituality by setting aside, one by one, the cares and goals of normal living, ending in an emptiness that was not Zen, but Christian. This is illustrated beautifully in one of my own favorite sayings from Eusebius of Emesa:

We saw a man who had not entered into matrimony, and we learned not to marry. We saw a man who had nowhere to lay his head, and we learned to disdain all material things. We saw a man who walked along the roads, not in order to buy or possess anything, but in order to teach us to put aside our belongings. We saw a man who fasted in order to show us how to fast, not with words, but by example.[19]

There is a real spiritual immediacy in the desert-father stories, and those who were drawn out into the desert to live the monastic life experienced radical changes in their lives through their admirable quest for authentic personhood. Nouwen learned from Abbot John Eudes and the Cistercians that the desert fathers practiced a particular type of prayer that promised freedom. This was the contemplative practice that would be known in subsequent centuries as the Jesus Prayer, a repetition of a phrase, such as "Lord Jesus Christ, Son of God, have mercy on me, a sinner," in order to center the mind and free it from distractions and even thoughts. The repeated phrase acted as an anchor against the winds and tides of temptation and distraction. This prayer would become a fundamental feature of Eastern Christianity. By the time Henri began to explore these matters, the Jesus Prayer was best known through an Eastern spiritual classic called the *Way of the Pilgrim*, the diary of an anonymous Russian peasant.[20]

Merton had not been able to do more than begin to unearth the wisdom traditions of the desert fathers. Fr. John Eudes, Henri's director, was taking Merton's explorations further through an investigation of Evagrius Ponticus, the great desert father theologian and theorist.[21] In the years when Henri was with John Eudes, the latter was busy with the translation and study of some of the basic works of this unknown spiritual giant. Because of the time he spent with John Eudes, Henri was exposed to the Evagrian idea that "thoughts" can be detrimental to one's focus on God, and so he began to incorporate this spiritual insight into his prayers and writings from the monastery. In *The Genesee Diary* he wrote:

> I have a strong feeling that my intellectual formation is just as much a hindrance as a help to prayer. It is hard not to desire good insights during prayer and not to fall into a long inner discussion with myself. Every time some kind of insight comes to me, I find myself wondering how I can use it in a lecture, a sermon, or an article, and very soon I am far away from God and all wrapped up in my own preoccupations. Maybe this is what makes the Jesus Prayer so good for me. Simply saying, "Lord Jesus Christ, have mercy on me" a hundred times, a thousand times, ten thousand times, as the Russian peasant did, might slowly clean my mind and give God a little chance.[22]

Nouwen's time in the monastery was the period of the most intense engagement of his life with the issue of prayer, and with the mental and emotional issues that are part of the life of prayer. It was a time of new realism, of facing his inabilities and his woundedness, and he emerged from his monastic experience a changed person. He realized he was not cut out for monastic life, but he had learned so much in the monastery that the experience stayed with him for many years. For some time he tried to be a monk in the world. He took on the practice of wearing the same simple clothes every day, and he tried to foster the Liturgy of the Hours, the Jesus Prayer, and community meals wherever he happened to be. If guests visited him, they were always invited to join him for prayer at the appointed hour.

As Henri Nouwen moved on—to Latin America, and to Harvard University, and into his l'Arche experience—faithfulness to prayer and to simplicity still continued to be a struggle for him. He was never satisfied with the way he was praying or how he was living. Thus, when he had the opportunity once to speak to Mother Teresa about his life, the simple words she spoke to him had a great impact, almost like the encounters in the desert father stories, in which the old monks were asked for a "word" by their young disciples. Here is his account of the experience:

> Once, quite a few years ago, I had the opportunity of meeting Mother Teresa of Calcutta. I was struggling with many things at the time and decided to use the occasion to ask Mother Teresa's advice. As soon as we sat down I started explaining all my problems and difficulties— trying to convince her of how complicated it all was! When, after ten minutes of elaborate explanation, I finally became silent, Mother Teresa looked at me quietly and said: "Well, when you spend one hour a day

adoring your Lord and never do anything which you
know is wrong . . . you will be fine!"

When she said this, I realized, suddenly, that she had
punctured my big balloon of complex self-complaints
and pointed me far beyond myself to the place of real
healing. In fact, I was so stunned by her answer that I
didn't feel any desire or need to continue the conversation. The many people waiting outside the room to
see her could probably use her time better than I. So I
thanked her and left. Her few words became engraved
on my heart and mind and remain to this day. I had
not expected these words, but in their directness and
simplicity, they cut though to the center of my being. I
knew that she had *spoken* the truth and that I had the
rest of my life to *live* it.[23]

This encounter bore much fruit in Henri's life. He needed
to be reminded periodically that actually praying was more important than speaking or writing about prayer. In the same way,
he needed to be reminded that living in community was more
important than speaking or writing about community. Living
these things out was all the more difficult because his highest
spiritual experience was in writing and in creating a vision to
show to others. Nevertheless, he took Mother Teresa's advice
and did make a sustained effort to pray every day for at least an
hour in total. He also said Mass daily. Thus, at l'Arche he
achieved a bit of needed regularity and as much peace as he was
likely to find. When I visited him there several years after he
left Harvard, I sensed a real difference in him.

There was one final stage in Henri's personal journey of
prayer. It is very common in the spiritual life to learn something and then be forced to forget or even unlearn it. After
decades—indeed a lifetime—devoted to learning to pray and
the special techniques of prayer, Henri was led by his pastoral

experience at l'Arche to move beyond his monastic experience and the Jesus Prayer to a very intense and simple experience of God and prayer in community. As he prayed with the handicapped members of l'Arche and their assistants, his many years of teaching spirituality in the classroom and learning to stay focused on God in the monastery—all the books and all the learning—began to matter less and less. All of that had been so much about what was in his head, and l'Arche, he realized, was not about the head, but the heart. Anyone with a heart can pray, and for a handicapped person to draw a simple cross or a star that gets put up on the wall is just as fine a prayer as any that Henri Nouwen ever composed for one of his publications.

The unlearning of the art of prayer that Henri Nouwen achieved at l'Arche, the move from prayer books to potatoes and to some very simple but wonderful people was the final step on a long and rich journey. In the final stages of the life of prayer, prayer becomes life, inseparable from breathing, as the Jesus Prayer teaches. It certainly happened that way for Nouwen.

Henri reached this final goal. Of course, he was not perfect or enlightened at the end of his life. There are always new vistas ahead of all of us, but, by learning and unlearning so much about prayer, he had come full circle. In the end, as he hovered near death in Holland, he said, "I don't think I am going to die, but if I do, tell everyone I am very grateful."

He did die that night. His death was somehow shocking, but not surprising. In the last few years he had had twice been near to death, once because of an accident, once because of an illness.[24] When I specifically asked him about taking care of his health, he told me, "I'm so old now, none of that matters any more." In my opinion, and that of many friends, for many years he was teetering on the edge of exhaustion. Ultimately, he worked himself to death. He had found the way, even while he was on sabbatical, to overtax himself with people and projects and writing. He lived so intensely that he burned himself out.

On a visit to his room during his sabbatical, I found a small candle lit on the writing desk where he had been sitting. I think about that candle often. There was Henri's artistic, aesthetic side again. The flame was also symbolic. Henri himself was like one big candle, casting so much light that he himself was ultimately consumed. I count him as one of the most fascinating and important people I have ever met. He bore the weight of a great charism. At the same time, he flew to impressive heights because he had been touched by that purifying gift of fire and spirit that rose from the burning bush and from the first Christians at Pentecost. This was a Dutchman who flew with God's angels.

The ministry of Henri Nouwen must be regarded by us today in the same way the first Christians regarded the baptism of John, as both a sign of God's presence . . . and of great things to come.

CONCLUSION

I feel a sense of gratitude and closure as I bring this book to an end. The contradictions of Henri's life will never be resolved completely, because they were so much a part of his wonderful reality. However, I hope that at this point in our journey together Henri doesn't seem as mystifying or puzzling as he did before. I have learned a great deal by writing this little book about Henri Nouwen, and I hope you have learned something by reading it to the end.

For myself at least, the Nouwen legacy seems to be entering a new phase. When Henri died I was initially devastated. In fact, I have never mourned anyone's passing as I did Henri's. After the initial shock subsided, I was very moved by all the tributes and other things people wrote about Henri. I also found I had a real need to explore the questions that I have tried to answer in this book. I say I have a sense of closure now, but perhaps that may prove illusory. When Henri died, I went up and spoke to Henri's brother, Laurent, at the funeral to tell him how much I had learned from Henri. He replied, "Well, now his work with you is finished! So, just keep doing like he taught you and thanks so much for coming!" His words meant a lot to me, but Laurent was wrong, as it turned out, because Henri's work with me was not finished, and I am still learning things from him, even today. That's why I think the sense of closure I have now may only be temporary.

In reality, this book will probably raise as many questions as it resolves. For some people, the portrait I have created of Henri will contain enough surprises and debatable observations and conclusions that it could spark another round of discussion and debate. If this happens, then one of my main objectives will have been achieved. In order for us to lay claim to Henri's legacy and see it extended, we must find answers to some key questions and grasp the essence of Henri's person and his message. We need to see how that message fits with the gospel as we understand it and ask if Henri's expansion on some of the themes of the New Testament is legitimate and proper.

Expansions there will always be. Wine and bread, the two elements of the Eucharist, have one thing in common: both contain yeast, and the yeast causes them to grow and be transformed. The gospel also contains its own sort of yeast, and it is made alive, grows, and changes in the hands of persons such as Henri. Nouwen's message has gone out into the world, but it is destined to go farther still. It must reach more people, and it also must penetrate more deeply into the hearts of each of us who have been touched by it already. This will take time and prayer, and it will take some talking. Maybe this book will help a few of us to take the discussion one step further. We still do not know where this one man's message will ultimately lead.

I do hope that in seeking to explain Henri's origins, or his psychology, or his method, or his message, I have not "explained him away" for any potential reader. Henri's spirituality is not so much a problem to be taken apart and analyzed as a gift to be enjoyed. My purpose has certainly not been to show that Henri Nouwen had feet of clay. Instead of that Old Testament image, I would recall the New Testament image of a treasure in a clay vessel. Henri was as full of human frailties as he was of the Spirit. Indeed, it is difficult to think of another figure that so perfectly combined divine inspiration and colorful, crazy humanity. He was a treasure in a clay pot. God bless him.

As I finish writing this page, it is winter. Outside, everything is white or grey. There are even some patches and lines that are black. The sky is very low. However, I am inside, sitting close to the fiery warmth of a wood stove. As I sit and write, I think about Henri and all that he taught us. I also think about Henri's thousands of friends and readers all over the world. He has left a broad and beautiful legacy for all of us to enjoy.

On the mantelpiece over my wood stove are cards we have recently received, some of them from people who knew Henri. The most beautiful card is from Jutta Ayer, a friend of ours and a very close friend of Henri. Jutta's card is handmade; it is a photograph she has taken, probably at l'Arche Daybreak, of a sunflower in winter. The sunflower's grey head is bowed down, almost in prayer, and it is crowned with a white cap of snow. The Spirit is sleeping, but soon will awake. Below the picture Jutta has penciled these words:

> And Winter
> slumbering in the open air
> wears on her smiling face
> a dream of Spring.

Henri sleeps in the same ground where that sunflower stands vigil. He himself no longer walks or stands among us, but, like the seed that falls to the ground, he too waits for the spring, and also waits, someday soon, for a great harvest.

NOTES

Introduction

1. That book was *The Return of the Prodigal Son: A Meditation on Fathers, Brothers and Sons* (New York: Doubleday, 1992). See also *"O," The Oprah Magazine* (July–August, 2000).

2. The most complete and varied collection is Beth Porter, ed., *Befriending Life: Encounters with Henri Nouwen* (New York: Doubleday, 2001).

3. The relationship between Nouwen and Bratman is described at greater length in Henri Nouwen, *Life of the Beloved: Spiritual Living in a Secular World* (New York: Crossroad, 1982) 9–21 and in Fred Bratman, "Making Dreams Come True," in Porter, *Befriending Life*, 245–47.

4. Henri Nouwen, *Reaching Out: The Three Movements of the Spiritual Life* (New York: Doubleday, 1966).

5. Jurjen Beumer, *Henri Nouwen: A Restless Seeking for God* (New York: Crossroad, 1997).

6. Michael Ford, *Wounded Prophet: A Portrait of Henri J. M. Nouwen* (New York: Crossroad, 1999).

7. I have expressed my views of this book more fully in a review entitled "Flying with the Dutchman: A Review of Two Recent Books about Henri Nouwen," *Christian Spirituality Review* 7:2 (1999) 21–25.

8. Robert Jonas, *Henri Nouwen: Writings Selected with an Introduction by Robert Jonas* (Maryknoll, N.Y.: Orbis Books, 1998).

9. Deirdre LaNoue, *The Spiritual Legacy of Henri Nouwen* (New York: Continuum, 2000).

10. Ronald Rolheiser, *The Holy Longing: The Search for a Christian Spirituality* (New York: Doubleday, 1999) v.

11. Nouwen, *Life of the Beloved*, 44.

12. See James 1:22.

1. Origins and Early Influences

1. John A. Coleman, *The Evolution of Dutch Catholicism* (Berkeley, Calif.: University of California, 1978) 51.

2. J. van Laarhoven, "Een land vol kerktorens," *De Bazuin*, 1 April, 1973, quoted in Walter Goddijn, *The Deferred Revolution: A Social Experiment in Church Innovation in Holland, 1960–1970* (Amsterdam: Elsevier, 1975) 5.

3. Peter Naus, "A Man of Creative Contradictions," in Beth Porter, ed., *Befriending Life: Encounters with Henri Nouwen* (New York: Doubleday, 2001) 79.

4. Coleman, *The Evolution of Dutch Catholicism*, 66.

5. Henri Nouwen, *Can You Drink the Cup?* (Notre Dame, Ind.: Ave Maria, 1996) 15.

6. Speaking for the video, *Straight to the Heart: The Life of Henri Nouwen*, produced by Karen Pascal (Markham, Ontario: Windborne Productions, 2001).

7. Nouwen, *Can You Drink the Cup?* 14.

8. Speaking for the video, *Straight to the Heart.*

9. Ibid.

10. Louis ter Steeg, interviewed and quoted in Michael Ford, *Wounded Prophet: A Portrait of Henri J. M. Nouwen* (New York: Doubleday, 1999) 79.

11. Robert Durback, ed., *Seeds of Hope: A Henri Nouwen Reader*, 2nd ed. (New York: Doubleday, 1997) 24.

12. Coleman, *The Evolution of Dutch Catholicism*, 87.

13. Ibid., 2.

14. Nouwen, *Can You Drink the Cup?* 15.

15. Frederick Franck, *Exploding Church: From Catholicism to catholicism* (New York: Delacorte, 1968) 13–14.

16. Naus, "A Man of Creative Contradictions," 79–80.

17. Battista Mondin, *I grandi teologi del secolo ventesimo*, 2 vols. (Turin: Borla, 1969) 2:301.

18. H. C. J. Duijker, "Psychology in the Netherlands," in *The Corsini Encyclopedia of Psychology and Behavioral Science*, 3rd ed., 4 vols. (New York: Wiley, 2001) 3:1029–31.

19. Ford, *Wounded Prophet*, 88.

20. See Peter Homans, *Theology after Freud* (Indianapolis, Ind.: Bobbs-Merrill, 1970).

21. For Freudian thinking and influence, see Edward Erwin, *The Freud Encyclopedia: Theory, Therapy and Culture* (New York: Routledge, 2002). For a Christian critique, see Stanton Jones and Richard Butman, *Modern Psychotherapies: A Comprehensive Christian Appraisal* (Downer's Grove, Ill.: Intervarsity, 1991) 65–91.

22. There is a vast literature on Jung and religion. For a good summary of Jungian theory, see Edward Whitmont, *The Symbolic Quest* (Princeton, N.J.: Princeton University, 1978). For a Christian response to Jung, see Antonio Moreno, *Jung, Gods, and Modern Man* (Notre Dame, Ind.: Notre Dame University, 1970), J. M. Spiegelman, *Catholicism and Jungian Psychology* (Phoenix, Ariz.: Falcon, 1988) and Wallace Clift, *Jung and Christianity* (New York: Crossroads, 1983). For a devastating critique of Jung's religiosity, see Richard Noll, *The Jung Cult: Origins of a Charismatic Movement* (Princeton, N.J.: Princeton University, 1994).

23. Jung's ambivalence toward religion is expressed clearly in the Terry Lectures on Religion delivered in 1938 at Yale University. See C. G. Jung, *Psychology and Religion* (New Haven, Conn.: Yale University, 1938).

24. Genesis 29:23.

25. Henri Nouwen, *Creative Ministry* (New York: Doubleday, 1971) xviii–xix.

26. Henri Nouwen, *In the Name of Jesus: Reflections on Christian Leadership* (New York: Crossroad, 1991) 42–44.

27. Henri Nouwen, "Anton Boisen and Theology Through Living Human Documents," *Pastoral Psychology* 19:186 (September 1968) 49–63.

28. Ford, *Wounded Prophet*, 89.

29. Duijker, "Psychology in the Netherlands," 1030.

30. John Dos Santos, "Remembering Henri," in Porter, *Befriending Life*, 196–97.

31. Goddijn, *The Deferred Revolution*.

32. A current review of Dutch pastoral psychology begins with the words: "Pastoral psychology is flourishing[!]." J. A. van Belzen, ed., *Op Weg naar Morgen: Godsdienstpsychologie in Nederland*, 2 vols.,

Studies op het terrain deer godsdienstpsychologie No. 8 (Kampen: Uitgeverij Kok, 2000) 2:7.

2. The Psychology of Henri Nouwen

1. Chris Glaser, *Henri's Mantle: 100 Meditations on Nouwen's Legacy* (Cleveland, Ohio: Pilgrim, 2002).

2. Michael Ford, *Wounded Prophet: A Portrait of Henri J. M. Nouwen* (New York: Crossroad, 1999).

3. *Straight to the Heart: The Life of Henri Nouwen*, a video produced by Karen Pascal (Markam, Ontario: Windborne Productions, 2001).

4. James Hillman, *The Soul's Code: In Search of Character and Calling* (New York: Random House, 1996).

5. Sue Erikson Bloland, "Fame: The Power and Cost of a Fantasy," *Atlantic Monthly* 284:5 (November 1999) 51–62.

6. Kathy Bruner, quoted in Ford, *Wounded Prophet*, 63.

7. The classic work on the *puer* is Marie-Louise von Franz, *The Problem of the Puer Aeternus*, 3rd ed. (Toronto: Inner City, 2000). The most important recent works on the *puer* are Jeffrey Satinover, "Puer Aeternus: The Narcissistic Relation to the Self," in *Quadrant* 13:2 (1980) and Ann Yeoman, *Now or Neverland: Peter Pan and the Myth of Eternal Youth* (Toronto: Inner City, 1998).

8. Henri Nouwen, *Beyond the Mirror* (New York: Crossroad, 1990) 53.

9. Thomas Moore and Joan Hanley, illustrator, *Original Self: Living with Paradox and Originality* (San Francisco: HarperCollins, 2000) 29.

10. Henri Nouwen, *The Return of the Prodigal Son: A Meditation on Fathers, Brothers and Sons* (New York: Doubleday, 1992).

11. After completing this chapter I was informed by Sr. Sue Mosteller that Henri had taken the MBTI and tested as ENFJ. Henri had a considerable amount of J in him, so this test result does not surprise me. However, I think that if Henri was tested on another occasion, his test result may have been ENFP. Because Henri was socialized in a predominantly J environment, I believe that his true P characteristics were often overshadowed. In what follows I hope to show that Henri matched the ENFP personality type rather closely, and that this was his true type.

12. Lenore Thomson, *Personality Type: An Owner's Manual* (Boston: Shambhala, 1998).

13. Ibid., 199–200.

14. Fred Rogers, "In the Journey, We Need Friends," in Christopher De Vinck, ed., *Nouwen Then: Personal Reflections on Henri* (Grand Rapids, Mich.: Zondervan, 1999) 77.

15. Michael O'Laughlin, "Flying with the Dutchman: A Review of Two Recent Books about Henri Nouwen," *Christian Spirituality Review* 7:2 (1999) 25.

16. Thomson, *Personality Type*, 204.

17. Ibid., 205–6.

18. Henri Nouwen, *Can You Drink the Cup?* (Notre Dame, Ind.: Ave Maria, 1996) 33–34.

19. Thomson, *Personality Type*, 206.

20. Henri Nouwen, *The Inner Voice of Love* (New York: Doubleday, 1996) 44.

21. Henri Nouwen, *In Memoriam* (Notre Dame, Ind.: Ave Maria, 1980) 16.

22. Elan Golomb, *Trapped in the Mirror: Adult Children of Narcissists in Their Struggle for Self* (New York: William Morrow, 1992). See also Alice Miller, *The Drama of the Gifted Child* (New York: Basic Books, 1981).

23. Personal correspondence with the author, dated 10/27/01, corrected for English language style.

24. The most readable book to appear on male homosexuality is J. Michael Bailey, *The Man Who Would Be Queen: The Science of Gender-Bending and Transsexualism* (Washington, D.C.: Joseph Henry, 2003).

25. The Judeo-Christian argument against homosexuality is well presented in Jeffrey Satinover, *Homosexuality and the Politics of Truth* (Grand Rapids, Mich.: Baker, 1996).

26. Peter Naus, "A Man of Creative Contradictions," in Beth Porter, ed., *Befriending Life: Encounters with Henri Nouwen* (New York: Doubleday, 2001) 85.

27. Naus, quoted in Ford, *Wounded Prophet*, 84.

28. Henri Nouwen, *Here and Now: Living in the Spirit* (New York: Crossroad, 1994) 77–78.

29. The classic formulation of this theory is found in two works by Erik Erikson, *Childhood and Society* (New York: Norton, 1963) and *Identity: Youth and Crisis* (New York: Norton, 1968). For a recent

adaptation, see George Vaillant, *The Wisdom of the Ego* (Cambridge, Mass.: Harvard University, 1993) 144–45.

30. Personal correspondence with the author dated 10/27/01, corrected for English language style.

31. 1 Corinthians 1:27; 2 Corinthians 13:4; 2 Corinthians 12:10.

32. Henri Nouwen, *Bread for the Journey: A Daybook of Wisdom and Faith* (HarperSanFrancisco, 1997) April 14.

3. An Artist, Not a Scribe

1. Henri Nouwen, *Behold the Beauty of the Lord: Praying with Icons* (Notre Dame, Ind.: Ave Maria, 1987).

2. Of course, Michelangelo was not the originator of this image. The *Pietà* arose out of centuries of meditation on the Passion of Christ. *Pietà* sculptures first appeared in German monastic circles around 1300. For a history of this spiritual art form, see Gertrud Schiller, *Iconography of Christian Art*, trans. Janet Seligman, 3 vols. (Greenwich, Conn.: New York Graphic Society, 1971) 2:179-81.

3. Henri Nouwen, *Lifesigns: Intimacy, Fecundity, and Ecstasy in Christian Perspective* (New York: Doubleday, 1966).

4. Ibid., 23.

5. John 14:23.

6. John 14:7

7. John 1:14.

8. John 1:38–39.

9. Henri Nouwen, *Lifesigns*, 88.

10. Henri Nouwen, *The Return of the Prodigal Son: A Meditation on Fathers, Brothers and Sons* (New York: Doubleday, 1992) 76.

11. Daniel 5:1–31.

12. Michael Ford, *Wounded Prophet: A Portrait of Henri J. M. Nouwen* (New York: Doubleday, 1999) xii.

13. Jurgen Beumer, *Henri Nouwen: A Restless Seeking for God* (New York: Crossroad, 1997) 24.

14. Cliff Edwards, *Van Gogh and God: A Creative Spiritual Quest* (Chicago: Loyola University, 1989) 44.

15. Letter 161, quoted in Edwards, *Van Gogh and God*, 48.

16. Henri Nouwen, *Sabbatical Journey: The Diary of His Final Year* (New York: Crossroad, 1998) 34.

17. The vast perspective of Thomas Merton is indicated by an encyclopedia dedicated to him: William Shannon, Christine Bocken, Patrick O'Connell, eds., *The Thomas Merton Encyclopedia* (Maryknoll, N.Y.: Orbis Books, 2002).

18. Thomas Merton, *New Seeds of Contemplation* (Norfolk, Conn.: New Directions, 1961) 1–2.

19. Henri Nouwen, *The Road to Peace: Writings on Peace and Justice*, ed. John Dear (Maryknoll, N.Y.: Orbis Books, 1998) 196–97.

20. Edwards, *Van Gogh and God*, 28, 56–57.

4. Eating and Drinking in the House of God

1. Henri Nouwen, *Can You Drink the Cup?* (Notre Dame, Ind.: Ave Maria, 1996).

2. Henri Nouwen, *Lifesigns: Intimacy, Fecundity, and Ecstasy in Christian Perspective* (New York: Doubleday, 1989) 122–23.

3. Henri Nouwen, *With Burning Hearts: A Meditation on the Eucharistic Life* (Maryknoll, N.Y.: Orbis Books, 1994) 65–66.

4. Nancy Krueger of Menasha, Wis., who added her comment to the Nouwen Literary Centre website (nouwen.org) on Tuesday, May 29, 2001.

5. For the remarks of Fred Rogers, see "In the Journey, We Need Friends," in Christopher De Vinck, ed., *Nouwen Then: Personal Reflections on Henri* (Grand Rapids, Mich.: Zondervan, 1999) 78.

6. Jean Vanier, "A Gentle Instrument of a Loving God," in Beth Porter, ed., *Befriending Life: Encounters with Henri Nouwen* (New York: Doubleday, 2001) 262–63.

7. Nouwen, *With Burning Hearts*, 65–66.

8. Ibid., 67.

5. Jesus at the Center

1. Mark Hatfield, in the foreword to Henri Nouwen, *With Open Hands* (New York: Ballantine, 1972) vii.

2. Henri Nouwen, *Beyond the Mirror* (New York: Crossroad, 1990) 47.

3. Henri Nouwen, *Letters to Marc about Jesus* (New York: HarperCollins, 1987) 7.

4. Henri Nouwen, *The Road to Daybreak* (New York: Doubleday, 1988) 22.

5. John 15:18–19.

6. Nouwen, *Letters to Marc*, 44–45.

7. Gustavo Gutiérrez, *We Drink from Our Own Wells: The Spiritual Journey of a People* (Maryknoll, N.Y.: Orbis Books, 1984).

8. This is Nouwen's message in *In the Name of Jesus: Reflections on Christian Leadership* (New York: Crossroad, 1991).

9. Romans 6:4.

10. John Dos Santos, "Remembering Henri," in Beth Porter, ed., *Befriending Life: Encounters with Henri Nouwen* (New York: Doubleday, 2001) 198.

11. Interviewed on the video by Karen Pascal, *Straight to the Heart: The Life of Henri Nouwen* (Markham, Ontario: Windborne Productions, 2001).

12. James Hillman, "Peaks and Vales," in James Hillman et al., *Puer Papers* (Irving, Tex.: Spring 1979) 65.

13. Mary Bastedo, "Henri and Daybreak, A Story of Mutual Transformation," in Porter, *Befriending Life*, 28.

14. Nouwen preached a televised sermon from the Crystal Cathedral that focused on this theme. That sermon's highlights, along with commentary by a panel, can be seen in a film called *Henri Nouwen's Passion and Spirituality* (Notre Dame, Ind.: Center for Social Concerns, University of Notre Dame, 2001).

15. Henri Nouwen, *The Return of the Prodigal Son: A Meditation on Fathers, Brothers and Sons* (New York: Doubleday, 1992) 50.

16. Ibid., 35–36.

17. 1 Corinthians 11:1.

18. Galatians 3:27.

19. Romans 8:29.

20. 1 John 3:1.

21. Henri Nouwen, *Life of the Beloved: Spiritual Living in a Secular World* (New York: Crossroad, 1992) 25–26.

22. 2 Corinthians 5:19.

23. Henri Nouwen, *Bread for the Journey: A Daybook of Wisdom and Faith* (HarperSanFrancisco, 1997) June 2–6.

24. Ibid., August 1.

25. *Adam: God's Beloved* (Maryknoll, N.Y.: Orbis Books, 1997) was published posthumously. It was edited and put in final form by Sue Mosteller, CSJ, Nouwen's literary executrix, to whom we owe a great debt of gratitude.

26. Ibid., 29–30.

27. The desert fathers lived alone, like hermits. The cenobites were those monks who lived in larger communities.

28. Benedicta Ward, *The Sayings of the Desert Fathers: The Alphabetical Collection* (Kalamazoo, Mich.: Cistercian Publications, 1975) 85; this is the second saying of Abba Isaac.

29. Henri Nouwen, *The Way of the Heart* (New York: Ballantine, 1981).

30. Nouwen, *Adam*, 69–70.

31. Ibid., 15–16.

6. Spirituality and Prayer

1. See p. 13 above.

2. One good example of the MBTI's use in spiritual direction is Charles Keating's *Who We Are Is How We Pray* (Mystic, Conn.: Twenty-Third Publications, 1987).

3. Chester Michael and Marie Norrisey, *Prayer and Temperament: Different Prayer Forms for Different Personality Types* (Charlottesville, Va.: Open Door, 1991) 59–60.

4. The best translation of Augustine's *Confessions* is that of F. J. Sheed, *Confessions of St. Augustine* (London and New York: Sheed & Ward, first published in 1944).

5. Peter Brown, *Augustine of Hippo* (New York: Dorset Press, 1986) 158–81. For a complete discussion of Augustine's spirituality, see Bernard McGinn, *The Foundations of Mysticism: Origins to the Fifth Century*, vol. 1 of The Presence of God: A History of Western Christian Mysticism (New York: Crossroad, 1994) 228–62.

6. These general groups are the Ignatian (SJ), the Augustinian (NF), the Franciscan (SP), and the Thomistic (NT).

7. Michael and Norrisey, *Prayer and Temperament*, 63.

8. Ibid., 61.

9. For three years Donald Nicholl was the rector of the Tantur

Ecumenical Institute near Jerusalem. His spiritual writings include *The Testing of Hearts: A Pilgrim's Journal* (London: Lamp Press, 1989), *Triumphs of the Spirit in Russia* (London: Darton, Longman and Todd, 1997), and *The Beatitude of Truth* (London: Darton, Longman and Todd, 1997).

10. Donald Nicholl, *Holiness*, 2nd ed. (London: Darton, Longman and Todd, 1997).

11. See above, p. 70.

12. Henri Nouwen, *Jesus and Mary: Finding Our Sacred Center* (Cincinnati, Ohio: St. Anthony Messenger Press, 1993) 9–10.

13. Henri Nouwen, *Letters to Marc about Jesus* (San Francisco: HarperCollins, 1998) 67–78.

14. M. Basil Pennington, "Three Spiritual Ways," in *Encyclopedic Dictionary of Religion*, 3 vols. (Washington, D.C.: Corpus Publications, 1979) 3:3718.

15. Luke 18:1–5.

16. Henri Nouwen, *The Only Necessary Thing: Living a Prayerful Life*, ed. Wendy Wilson Greer (New York: Crossroad, 1999).

17. Martin Buber, *I and Thou*, ed. and trans. Walter Kaufmann (New York: Simon & Schuster, 1970, 1996).

18. Thomas Merton, *The Wisdom of the Desert* (New York: New Directions, 1960) 5–6.

19. E. M. Buytaert, *Eusèbe d'Emèse, Discours conservés en latin* (Louvain: Spicilegium sacrum lovaniense 26, 1953) 1:180–81.

20. R. M. French, *The Way of the Pilgrim* (New York: Seabury, 1965).

21. For an excellent overview of this topic, see Kallistos Ware, "Ways of Prayer and Contemplation, I. Eastern," in Bernard McGinn, John Meyendorff, and Jean Leclerq, *Christian Spirituality, Origins to the Twelfth Century*, vol. 16 of World Spirituality: An Encyclopedic History of the Religious Quest (New York: Crossroad, 1985) 395–415.

22. Henri Nouwen, *The Genesee Diary: Report from a Trappist Monastery* (New York: Doubleday, 1976) 104.

23. Henri Nouwen, *Here and Now: Living in the Spirit* (New York: Crossroad, 1994) 88.

24. Henri Nouwen, *Beyond the Mirror* (New York: Crossroad, 1990).